Objects of Bright Pride

NORTHWEST COAST INDIAN ART FROM THE AMERICAN MUSEUM OF NATURAL HISTORY

It is easy to become entranced by the soft curtain of age, seeing this instead of what it obscures. An ugly building can make a beautiful ruin, and a beautiful mask in the dark of many years, softened by wear, becomes a symbol which tells us that the cycle of life, death, decay and rebirth is a natural and beautiful one.

This is not what their creators intended. These were objects of bright pride, to be admired in the newness of their crisply carved lines, the powerful flow of sure elegant curves and recesses—yes, and in the brightness of fresh paint. They told the people of the completeness of their culture, the continuing lineages of the great families, their closeness to the magic world of universal myth of legend.

WILLIAM REID / 1967

Allen Wardwell

Objects of Bright Pride

NORTHWEST COAST INDIAN ART FROM THE AMERICAN MUSEUM OF NATURAL HISTORY

The Center for Inter-American Relations

and

The American Federation of Arts

cover illustration
35.
**POTLATCH TRANSFORMATION
MASK, KWAKIUTL**

The Center for Inter-American Relations
conducts educational programs in the visual arts, music, literature and
public affairs in order to enlarge our knowledge and appreciation of the
cultural heritage as well as the political, economic and social problems of
the Western Hemisphere.

The American Federation of Arts
is a national, non-profit, educational organization, founded in 1909, to
broaden the knowledge and appreciation of the arts of the past and present. Its primary activities are the organization of exhibitions which travel
throughout the United States and abroad, and the fostering of a better
understanding among nations by the international exchange of art.

©1978 The Center for Inter-American Relations and The American Federation of Arts

Published by
The Center for Inter-American Relations
680 Park Avenue
New York, New York 10021
and
The American Federation of Arts
41 East 65th Street
New York, New York 10021
AFA Exhibition No. 78-19
Distributed by the University of Washington Press,
Seattle & London
ISBN 0-295-95664-X
Distributed in Canada by Douglas & McIntyre,
Vancouver
ISBN 0-88894-259-1

Library of Congress Catalogue Number 78-67113
Designed by Leon Auerbach
Photographs by Bob Hanson
Typography by Unbekant Typo Inc.
Printed by The Arts Publisher, Inc., Richmond & New York.
Printed in U.S.A.

ALASKA

Yakutat Bay

Chilkat River

TLINGIT

Indians of the Northwest Coast

ADMIRALTY
ISLAND

Sitka •

Prince of
Wales Island

TSIMSHIAN

Nass River

CANADA

Prince Rupert •

Skeena River

HAIDA

Queen
Charlotte
Islands

BELLA BELLA

BELLA COOLA

Bella Coola River

MILBANK
SOUND

Queen
Charlotte
Sound

KWAKIUTL

Pacific Ocean

Nootka
Sound

CAPE COOK

Vancouver
Island

UNITED STATES

This exhibition and publication have been supported by a grant from the National Endowment for the Arts.

Participating Museums

Cleveland Museum of Art
The Denver Art Museum
Museum of Natural History of Los Angeles County
Seattle Art Museum
New Orleans Museum of Art
Center for Inter-American Relations, New York

Contents

Objects of Bright Pride

1.
FACE MASK, KWAKIUTL
wood, brass, nails, fiber, black,
red and green pigment,
52.2 cm. h.

Collected by G. Hunt in 1902.
Boas gives the name of this
mask as kwexagila. *Certain*
areas of this mask have recently
been restored.

In fulfillment of its mandate to present to U.S. audiences art from all other nations of the Western Hemisphere, the Center for Inter-American Relations maintains a continuing interest in the traditional as well as in the contemporary art of Canada. For some years, therefore, we have followed with enthusiasm the resurgence of popularity in the U.S. of the spectacular objects made by Indians of the Northwest Coast of Canada and the United States, and wondered how we might make our own contribution to the furtherance of study and public knowledge in this field.

The answer came serendipitously. Soon after Allen Wardwell became Director of the Asia House Gallery in New York City, a conversation with him included mention of *Yakutat South*, an exhibition of Northwest Coast objects that he had organized in 1964, during his previous role as Curator of Primitive Art at the Art Institute of Chicago. Asked whether there was sufficient Northwest Coast material still unknown to the general public to warrant a new exhibition, Mr. Wardwell replied affirmatively—and added that he would be glad to research the subject further as guest curator.

Concurrently, the Center joined forces with The American Federation of Arts, which began inquiries around the national museum community to see what interest there might be in an exhibition that would be seen not only in New York but also elsewhere in the nation. Positive responses came quickly.

Mr. Wardwell, meanwhile, concentrated his attention on the substantial collection at The American Museum of Natural History. Millions of visitors had over the years walked by the large Northwest Coast war canoe just inside the Museum's 77th Street entrance, and into the large permanent display in the adjacent hall. But few were aware of the quantity and quality of the additional material in the Museum's storerooms — a reserve that includes many magnificent pieces that have never been seen by the public, nor photographed for publication. A selection from this little known resource was completed and permission secured for the loan of 100 works.

Proud as we are to present this exhibition, we are also humbly aware of the many talents and decisions needed to make our idea a reality. Allen Wardwell's enthusiasm and expertise were, naturally, of primary importance. We also appreciate the courtesy of Phillips Talbot, President of the Asia Society, in allowing Mr. Wardwell to allocate part of his time to the project. Two members of the Asia House Gallery staff also gave generously of their time and skill. Assistant Director Sarah Bradley edited the manuscripts of the catalogue essays and secretary Carol Lew Wang typed initial notes and data into their proper form.

At the American Museum of Natural History, we must also highlight the support for this project of Dr. Thomas N. Nicholson, Director, and the invaluable assistance of Dr. Philip C. Gifford, Scientific Assistant in the Anthropology Department. Dr. Gifford saw through the paperwork connected with the loan, supervised the restoration and preparation of the objects for travel and patiently worked with Mr. Wardwell in supplying information on the collection and its history and gave helpful criticism of parts of the original manuscript. We would also like to thank Dr. David Hurst Thomas, Associate Curator and Chairman of the Anthropology Department, Ann Metcalfe, Manager of Department of Public Affairs and Development and Anibal Rodriguez, Curatorial Assistant for their cooperation. If the exhibition we have assembled helps to illustrate to national audiences the scale and importance of this Museum's collections, this is only a small way of thanking them for enabling us to put it together.

We would also like to acknowledge the valuable guidance of the Center's Visual Arts Advisory Committee, and to thank the following staff members of the two sponsoring organizations: James B. Wolfe, Director, Sharon L. Schultz, Assistant to the Director, Mara E. Gardner, Education Coordinator and Esteban Perez, Installation Consultant of the Center for Inter-American Relations; Jane S. Tai, Associate Director for Program, Susanna D'Alton, Coordinator of Exhibitions, Melissa Meighan, Registrar, Mary Ann Monet, Assistant to the Registrar and Konrad G. Kuchel, Coordinator of Loans of The American Federation of Arts.

Thanks are also due to Leon Auerbach for designing the catalogue and related graphics, and to Bob Hanson for the catalogue photography.

Finally, we cannot fail to express our deep appreciation to the National Endowment for the Arts for its generous support of both the publication and the exhibition.

Roger D. Stone, *President*
Center for
Inter-American Relations

Wilder Green, *Director*
The American Federation
of Arts

Northwest Coast Indian art is one of the most distinctive of all the arts of man. When one has come to know the components of this dynamic style, it is impossible to confuse it with art from any other part of the world. Because almost all of the materials which were used for the art are subject to decay, there is little or no archaeology which would help us to understand how such an extraordinary graphic and sculptural expression might have evolved. Wood, the principal medium, and such other materials used as horn, bone, walrus ivory, shell, animal hide, and wool did not survive long periods of use or exposure to the northern rain forest environment of this part of the world.

The objects that remain, such as those presented here, were almost all made within the last two centuries. Although there are a few stone bowls and ivory and bone sculptures that might have been created at earlier times, it is impossible to know exactly how old they are. Concerning origin, certain relationships between Northwest Coast art and the nomadic art of the northern steppes of Asia have been suggested; intriguing similarities have also been noted between Northwest Coast design and some of the arts of the Pacific Basin and early China. These parallels have given rise to numerous controversial theories of contact and outside influence from Asia and parts of the Pacific. It is not the purpose of this essay to examine the various theories that have been put forth about the background of the Northwest Coast style. We should not, however, be surprised to find a certain correspondence between this art and some of the arts of Asia. The people of the Northwest Coast originally migrated there from Asia, coming across the Bering Straits. There was probably also some continuing though intermittent contact with the east throughout the existence of the Indian culture. In historic times, a number of vessels were blown off course to the coast from Asia and similar incidents must have occurred earlier as well. Whatever its sources, the art of the Northwest Coast developed to become a unique expression and style. Over the past century, it has caught the imagination and fascination of art historian and anthropologist alike.

The Northwest Coast is one of the richest natural environments in the world. It is a thin strip of land stretching along the Pacific from Yakutat Bay, Alaska, to Puget Sound, Washington. Coves, bays, inlets, large rivers and thousands of islands break up the storms of the Pacific and provide natural shelter and protection. The Japanese current which sweeps by the entire coast causes much rain and fog, but also prevents the extreme cold which ordinarily would exist at this northern latitude. This current also nurtures a wealth of marine life in the form of shellfish, waterfowl, seagoing mammals and fish. The abundant salmon runs were particularly important to the stability of the Indian culture, because in the space of a few weeks during the summer months, enough food could be harvested and put up to feed the inhabitants for the remainder of the year. Thus freed from the demands of day to day survival, the Indians of the Northwest Coast had time for the development and enactment of elaborate ceremonies and for the creation and manufacture of the objects that were to be used with them.

The land provided as much wealth as the sea.

The massive trees that grow in the coastal forests such as red and yellow cedar, fir, spruce and alder were split, steamed, carved and shredded to serve a wide variety of purposes. Wood was made into houses, canoes, boxes, storage chests, masks, implements and many other ceremonial and utilitarian objects. Spruce roots were woven into basketry, and often used to sew the bottoms and sides of boxes together. Fibers of cedar bark were softened, shredded and then woven into articles of clothing. In addition, such land animals as mountain sheep and goats, bear, deer, beaver, otter, and ermine supplied food and material for clothing and ornamentation.

Because there was almost no agriculture, subsistence was attained almost entirely from fishing, hunting and gathering. Such methods of survival often only allow the simplest and most primitive forms of society and culture to develop, but the natural abundance of the environment easily filled the basic needs for food, shelter and clothing. It has been said that the Northwest Coast Indians attained the highest development of any culture ever to exist without the benefits of agriculture and animal domestication. There was, in fact, such a natural wealth on the Northwest Coast that some ceremonies were developed in which certain types of property and food were actually burnt and destroyed at feasts. Such feasts, which were known as potlatches, were held to prove to the onlookers the great position of the host. Much of the ceremonial activity, and consequently the production of art of the Northwest Coast was directed towards maintaining or enhancing wealth and status, and the most important single factor that brought about the existence of these cultural traits was undoubtedly the character and richness of the environment.

The Indian peoples who lived along the coast and are represented here by their art comprised six major linguistic groups.[1] The northernmost area, consisting of the Alaskan panhandle from Yakutat Bay to Cape Fox, was inhabited by the Tlingit. Directly to the south, occupying Queen Charlotte Island and the southern end of Prince of Wales Island, lived the Haida. The mainland and islands to the east of Queen Charlotte Island was occupied by the Tsimshian, whose villages were mostly situated on the Nass and Skeena Rivers. To the south, the land was inhabited by three groups, the Kwakiutl, the Bella Bella and the Bella Coola. The most numerous of these were the Kwakiutl who lived on the coast from the area of the Gardner and Douglas Channels down to the northern part of Vancouver Island as far south as Cape Cook. The Bella Bella, often considered a sub-group of the Kwakiutl, also lived on the northern part of Vancouver Island around Milbank Sound. The closely related Bella Coola inhabited the mainland to the northeast, around the Dean and Burke Channels and along the lower Bella Coola River.

This very general description refers only to the areas occupied by the peoples as they came to be known in the nineteenth century, not to the many migrations and shifts in population that occurred earlier. These were brought about by the expansion of stronger groups over smaller and less well established ones. Studies of the art and culture of the Indians who lived to the south of the Kwakiutl are often

In 1881, photographer Edward Dossetter accompanied Israel W. Powell on an inspection tour of the Northwest Coast, going as far north as Wrangell. Dossetter made a number of well-known views of Haida and Kwakiutl villages as well as landscapes of mountains and glaciers. Powell probably collected a number of objects for H. R. Bishop during the time of this tour. Haida Indians at the village of Masset, Queen Charlotte Island. Photograph, Edward Dossetter, 1881.

included in catalogues and exhibitions of this kind. In appearance and use, however, the art of such peoples as the Nootka, the Salish and the Makah is only peripherally related to that of the six northern tribes and is therefore not incorporated in this exhibition.

Although some examples of Northwest Coast art were purely utilitarian in their purpose, most of the art was made for heraldic display, for complex secret society initiation rites, or to represent certain spirit alliances on which a shaman would rely for magic and power in ceremonies which he performed. In the first category, the art reaches its most spectacular and monumental forms. Such creations as totem poles, house posts, grave markers, painted house fronts and interior screens, gigantic feast dishes and large carved and painted canoes were all made to impress those who saw them with the ancestry, status and wealth of their owners. In addition, smaller objects and examples of decorative art were made and used to serve similar purposes. Ceremonial costumes, headdresses, helmets, speakers' staffs, certain types of rattles, serving implements, eating utensils and boxes and containers of various kinds were carved, painted and often inlaid to depict various animal symbols that represent inherited clan emblems. The most important of these are the raven, the bear, the wolf, the eagle and the frog. However, practically any animal that existed on the land or in the waters of the Northwest Coast, from mosquitoes to whales can be found in the art, either appearing as a separate motif, or in sometimes extremely complex juxtapositions with other forms.

This rich decorative art, produced for social display, was most often used at elaborate winter potlatches. A wealthy chief might call a potlatch to announce the acquisition of a new title or crest, to celebrate a coming of age, or to repay a social obligation. The underlying motivation, however, was always to reassert and add to his status and position in the eyes of all who knew of him. Those who attended such feasts often traveled long distances, knowing that they themselves would lose status if they failed to participate. The houses in which these ceremonies were held were decorated with houseposts, painted screens and, on the outside, totem poles, all serving to call attention to the legendary background of their owners. Hereditary family myths and mythical encounters with spirits were reenacted in dramatic performances and dances. In this way, the manner in which a specific crest had become a chief's property was demonstrated to the assembled guests, and his ownership of it was thereby further substantiated. Masks of animal and human form, costumes and a wide variety of ceremonial regalia were created to be used in this context. The ceremonial dress worn by the chief and other members of his family, the implements he used to serve food, the boxes and containers in which his property was kept and from which it was distributed to the guests, and the eating utensils used by the guests were all decorated to call attention to his ancestry, greatness and wealth. As has already been mentioned, in some cases, property was destroyed at such ceremonies. Rival chiefs in attendance were obliged to give similar, often even more elaborate displays or suffer devastating loss of face.

Among the southern groups, particularly the Kwakiutl, there existed certain secret societies whose ceremonies also required a broad range of spectacular and often complex objects. Male adolescents were initiated into these societies after they had spent weeks or sometimes months in isolation outside the village. During the time they were away, they were thought to have become possessed by animal spirits. On their return, they behaved like wild animals and long ceremonies were enacted to bring about ritual taming so that they might be admitted to adult society. For these ceremonies, artists created masks and costumes which represented the animal spirits themselves as well as certain of their supernatural attendants and associates. Such additional ceremonial paraphernalia as rattles, drums, whistles, decorations and dress for dances were also made for these complex rituals. Secret society ceremonies served to bring the various forest, sea and animal spirits into closer contact with man and helped to renew his relationships with the pervasive supernatural world.

These spirits were not regarded as deities, but rather as manifestations of the forces of nature. Before the coming of man, they were thought to have inhabited the world. With the proper ceremonial ritual, spirit aid was sought for many purposes. The most powerful were spirits of the sky, mountains and glaciers, and of such animals as the bear, the land otter and the devilfish. They were called on to lend assistance to shamans who relied upon their alliances with the spirit world for their magic. Shamans were believed to have the power to do such things as foresee the future, heal the sick, exorcise evil spirits, bring success in fishing and hunting, and even control the weather. The assistance of many lesser spirits was also sought, and a particularly successful and powerful shaman had aid from certain spirits whose help could not be enlisted by any other.

Among some Northwest Coast groups a shaman would fast and spend long days in solitary vigil away from the village until a spirit finally revealed itself to him. Revelations would sometimes occur while he was in a trance. Once a bond had been established between a shaman and a spirit, the alliance could exist for life. The power of a shaman might sometimes exceed even that of a chief. Because they were in such close contact with the world of the supernatural they were greatly feared members of their community. Often a shaman lived in the forest, away from the village he served, and would only participate in the daily activities of his community if it did not interfere with his practice.

The equipment used by the shaman forms an important category of Northwest Coast art. Because its purpose is to substantiate a relationship with the supernatural, the art stands somewhat apart from the art made for crest display for chiefs and their families. Where the ceremonial equipment and masks used by secret societies is dramatic, and the art made for prestige display is decorative and often spectacular, the material used by the shaman has more of a magical and surrealistic quality to it, serving as it does to give form to an invisible world of spirits and supernatural beliefs.

Masks were an important part of a shaman's paraphernalia. Face masks representing mythical creatures might be worn by him or his helpers to impersonate the spiritual agency which was called on during a particular performance. At such times the shaman or his assistants became possessed by the spirit of the mask and his movements and actions were thought to be controlled by it. Miniature masks were also worn by the shaman on headdresses or sometimes sewn on aprons to further identify the spirit agent. Some of the most interesting carvings owned by the shaman were a variety of charms made of walrus ivory, bone, antler or animal teeth. These again represented spirits assisting the shaman. Almost all are in the form of mythical animals; some of the most important are carved to represent more than one spirit in complex juxtapositions and interrelations of forms. Rattles, noisemakers, drums, musical instruments, puppets and dolls, and crowns worn during practice were also part of the shaman's gear.

A shaman could inherit certain powers and spirits from his predecessor and might even use the masks, charms and costumes which had been passed on to him as heirlooms.[2] In certain instances, however, each object had its own meaning, and the power that existed in it could not be transferred to another. On his death, the body of a shaman was often placed in a grave house with the equipment that he had used.

The style of Northwest Coast art, while striking and highly original, is at the same time standardized and governed by strict and carefully observed rules of design. Numerous descriptions of the elements of Northwest Coast art have been written. Among the characteristics most frequently mentioned are bilateral symmetry, use of bold and contrasting colors, particularly red and black, the ''splitting'' and rearrangement of human or animal forms so that they cover the entire surface of an object and the exaggeration of certain distinguishing anatomical features such as beaks, claws, mouths and face types to identify specific animals. Bill Holm's *Northwest Coast Indian Art: An Analysis of Form*, published in 1965, represents an orderly, thoughtful study of the art that has become the standard reference for any description of this style. Holm coins the appropriate term ''formline'' to describe the single most significant element of Northwest Coast art, and the one which gives it its unmistakable appearance. This striking, flowing, almost calligraphic line is the one which delineates every unit of design. It is unique and pervasive to this art and besides being simply beautiful, it also gives a quality of inner life and dynamism to every object on which it appears.

Holm makes an interesting observation in noting the possible relationship between the nature of the formline and the movements of dance. His description of the formline itself, could, in fact, almost be taken for an analysis of a specific dance:

> Formlines swell and diminish, rarely retaining the same width for any distance. Generally they swell in the center of a given design unit and diminish at the ends. The width of a formline usually changes with a major change of direction. These changes in width are governed by the specific design unit formed and its relation to adjacent units.
>
> Formlines are essentially curvilinear. The curves are gentle and sweeping, breaking suddenly into semi-angular curves and, immediately upon completing the necessary direction change (usually around 90 degrees), straightening to a gentle curve again.[3]

This suggestion of the interrelationship of one art form to another is given further weight when we are told that some of the finest artists of the Kwakiutl were also the best dancers and song writers.

Holm divides the various types of formlines into four categories according to their importance in the overall design applied to an object, and then goes on to describe many other aspects of the art. These include the predominant use of the ovoid form, the sensitive relationship of any design to the space to be decorated, the quality of movement achieved through use of the curvilinear patterns and forms that flow into one another, and the double meaning of certain designs by which one form might also become part of a completely different being or animal. The principles governing the creation of two-dimensional Northwest Coast art are carried into three dimensions as well, both in relief carvings and in those fully in the round.

One of the most difficult problems encountered in the study of Northwest Coast two-dimensional art is the interpretation of certain designs. Many of the distinguishing characteristics of specific animal and human forms such as hands, fins, claws, flippers, beaks, feathers, teeth and mouth shapes can be easily identified and continually spring to our attention, but these elements are often rearranged to fit certain

The Haida village of Skidegate. Photograph, Maynard, c. 1885.

spaces or to conform to the demands of symmetry. To our eyes, such stylized designs are often unintelligible, and if we seek to identify a specific animal representation, we are often frustrated. Unfortunately, too, information about the meaning of a piece gathered at the time it was collected is often vague or even contradictory. The extreme abstraction of some of these patterns was dictated in part by the standardized and rigid rules of design that have already been mentioned. It is also possible, as has recently been suggested by Wilson Duff,[4] that some patterns may have been deliberately stylized. If true, the owner of the object on which they appear could have identified them to be any of a number of crest designs he owned and with which he could impress his guests.

Attribution of an object to a specific area or group is also difficult even if it is accompanied by accurate collection data. There are regional variations in the art which range from the more expressionistic, often bolder paintings and sculpture of the southern groups to the finer, more naturalistic carvings made in the north. Admittedly, this is an over-simplification of numerous subtle differences between one style and another which have been identified by scholars with some success. Because there was considerable exchange and communication between different families and tribes, however, certain stylistic distinctions become blurred, and it is often virtually impossible to examine a piece and give its tribal origin with absolute certainty.

Several types of objects and certain woodworking techniques were highly developed and distinctive to the Northwest Coast. One is the bent wood box, a common item used for storage of prestige materials, to serve food, and as a cooking vessel. The techniques of its manufacture, whereby the wood was bent around the square corners and pegged and sewn together, are described in the following catalogue notes. Manipulation of wood in this manner was a specialized achievement of these craftsmen. Some of the food and oil bowls were made with such skill that they are completely watertight.

The totem pole is another unique creation of this culture. Appropriately it has become the best-known single image of this art, because it represents, on a monumental scale, the Indians' overriding concern with status and ancestry. Totem poles were simply one of many ways for a family to display the ownership of specific crests. Usually these crests were inherited, and the number and importance of those claimed enhanced the position of the owners. Totem poles told family histories and how certain crests came to be owned through encounters with supernatural beings. Sometimes they also included references to successful competitions over rival chiefs. Other monumental carvings that are closely related to totem poles are mortuary poles erected near the graves of dead chiefs, house posts that decorated the interior of houses, and memorial poles that were put up by the heirs of chiefs to show that ownership of a predecessor's crests and titles had been assumed.

Many of the same principles of design and composition employed in the conception of the totem pole and these other monumental carvings were also applied to many of the smaller art objects of the Northwest Coast. The handles of the mountain goat

and sheep horn spoons are in appearance, purpose and significance, miniature totem poles themselves. Certain shaman's charms, although often carved to be seen horizontally, also consist of similar complex juxtapositions and interrelationships of animal forms and human figures. Masks, rattles, speakers' staffs, combs, pipes and dagger handles often share these characteristics as well. Textile designs and two-dimensional decorations are also extremely stylized compositions of many different human and animal beings. As an art form, the totem pole can thus be seen to share elements of design and conception that are found throughout the art.

Different animal and human spirits are also combined in a sculptural form developed by Northwest Coast artists that is even more spectacular and unusual than the totem pole. This is the type of mask known as the transformation mask. It was constructed so that it could be opened up to reveal the face of another animal, human, or supernatural being on its inside. In this way, the interrelationship of different spirits was revealed with great drama. Such masks were worn to illustrate myths of animal ancestry, to display various crests owned by a chief, or show the interaction of one spirit with another. The added dimension of motion and the dance rendered these works particularly effective. The wearer of the mask would move in a certain way when one part of the mask was being displayed and in another when the mask suddenly changed to depict a different form. Even in the static museum installations of today, these objects transmit much of the theatricality of Northwest Coast ceremony to us. When it is in actual use, ''the sudden 'blossoming' of

They were people of high culture, with a capable technology based on woodworking, an elaborate ceremonial life and a passion for making their social and religious worlds visible through the plastic and graphic arts.

WILSON DUFF/1967

such a mask never fails to draw gasps of amazement from the audience."[5]

This sense of drama and dynamism pervades each piece of Northwest Coast art. Although more easily recognized in the monumental and spectacular works such as the totem poles, transformation masks, house posts and painted house screens, the same qualities emerge from the smallest shaman's charm, spoon, or miniature mask. Present day artists and art historians have been captivated by the beautiful, pure and bold designs of these things. Anthropologists have become intrigued with the origins and development of such a rich iconography and the wonderful myths and legends that came from this society. Ethnographers have marveled over the great variety of the material culture.

Today, most of the ceremonies which caused these "objects of bright pride" to be created have ceased to exist. They are shown here removed from their natural and ritual environment, and the people who view them do not believe in them as their creators once did. Nonetheless, much of the vitality of this extraordinary culture is transmitted to us by these pieces. To be exposed to this art is to experience some of the intensity of Northwest Coast ceremony, to sense the presence of a world of supernatural spirits and the magic and power they controlled, and to feel the overpowering beauty, richness and mystery of this land and sea.

[1]*This information was adapted from* Indians of the Northwest Coast *by Philip Drucker, p. 9-16.*

[2]*See F. de Laguna's note on Tlingit shamans in National Gallery of Art, 1973, p. 227.*

[3]*Bill Holm, 1965, p. 37.*

[4]*Quoted by Holm in William Sturtevant's catalogue,* Boxes and Bowls, *p. 24.*

[5]*Bill Holm, 1972, p. 48.*

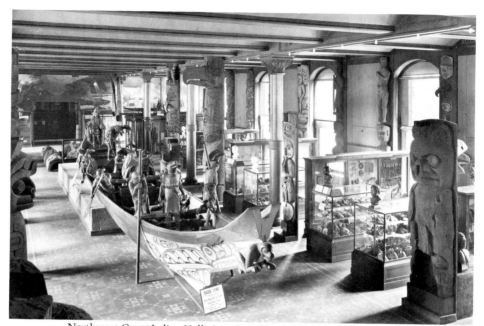

Northwest Coast Indian Hall, American Museum of Natural History, 1910.

Present installation, Northwest Coast Indian Gallery, American Museum of Natural History, 1962.

At the end of the nineteenth century, the Indian cultures of the Northwest Coast were in a state of final decline. The last great age of chiefs and shamans, which had actually been stimulated by the coming of the European, American and Russian traders a century earlier was being brought to an end by the imposition of a new, unfamiliar and ultimately incompatible culture. It would not be long before most of the fabulous feasts and ceremonies would cease to be held and shamans would no longer perform their cures or displays of magic and power. The incentives to create the spectacular monumental carvings and innumerable ritual and decorative works which have given this culture its great renown were fast disappearing.

Fortunately for later generations the period also coincided with the formation of several major museums in the United States and Canada. A few foresighted museum professionals and public spirited citizens realized that if any collections of this material were to be made, there was not much time to be wasted. A poignant description of the state of decay of a Haida village, written in 1878 by George Dawson, serves to foretell the immediate future of this woodcarving tradition and its artifacts:

> These permanent villages of the Haidas are now much reduced in number, in correspondence with the very rapid decrease of the people themselves. Those villages least favorably situated as fishing stations or most remote from communication have been abandoned. . . . Even those still occupied are rapidly falling to decay. . . . Many houses have been completely deserted while others are shut up and moldering away under the weather. . . . The carved posts, though one may still be erected, are as a rule, more or less advanced toward decay. A rank growth of weeds, in some cases presses close up among the inhabited houses. . . . In a few years, little of the original aspect of these villages will remain. . . .

Many similar observations evidently stimulated interest in preserving the remarkable sculptures of the Northwest Coast in museum collections.

The American Museum of Natural History was founded in 1869. Eleven years later, it set about to form what was to become one of the largest, most important and best documented collections of Northwest Coast art and ethnology in the world. The occasion is noted in the Annual Report of 1880: "Mr H.R. Bishop has arranged with Dr. J.W. Powell, Superintendent of Indian Affairs in British Columbia, to forward us as rapidly as they can be gathered, a complete series of ethnological specimens of that region, and has already presented a few valuable ornaments obtained at Victoria, Vancouver's Island." For this venture, not much money was required, even when one takes the value of the dollar in 1880 into consideration. Heber R. Bishop, a New York businessman, agreed to pay the costs of purchasing the objects, and the sum of $2,500 was sufficient for Powell to acquire a collection of 791 pieces that were shipped to the museum over the next three years. Bishop also paid curator Franz Boas $300 to catalogue the collection, a project Boas worked on in his spare time.

Israel W. Powell (who because of a quirk in his penmanship often appears in museum records and publications as J.W. Powell) was quick to recognize the moral dilemma in which his position as Superintendent of Indian Affairs placed him. Expressing his concern about the ethics of his acquisition activities, he wrote to Albert Bickmore, the president of the museum in 1882, "I should not like to undertake another work of this kind, and when looking at [the objects in the collection] this morning, I really felt guilty of a want of patriotism in sending the collection out of the country." Powell had actually collected some fine early pieces for the National Museum of Man at Ottawa in 1879, and could therefore be relieved of some of his guilt, but this statement is particularly interesting in the light of similar questions of acquisition policy that are being raised in the museum profession today.

Despite these pangs of conscience, Powell realized the importance of the material he had gathered together. In 1883 he wrote to Professor Bickmore, "I know you will be delighted with the collection as a whole, and I have no doubt that it will constitute one of the features of the museum." In 1885, he again wrote that such a collection "cannot be duplicated in the country, and I beg to congratulate the museum on its possession. Many of those [pieces] sent to you were culled from both collections made by me and were intended for retention here. However, during an absence of some months from home, I returned to find many of the articles so damaged by moths that I made up my mind to hand them all over to you."

The high quality of the material in the Bishop collection is represented by the 11 pieces from it that are included in this exhibition. One of the remaining 780 objects happens to be the best-known Northwest Coast carving in the entire museum. It is the great 64 foot 6 inch long Bella Bella canoe that has been at the 77th Street entrance of the museum since 1960. There is no record of what Powell paid for this remarkable object, but its shipment to New York did cause him some problems and concern. At the time it was placed on board the steamer *G.W. Elder*, bound from Victoria to San Francisco, Powell wrote, "I was fearful that in crossing, it would be exposed to the action of the sun and split, and I employed a ship carpenter to put in a number of ribs which I was advised would prevent it. I found considerable difficulty in getting any steamer to take it, and am therefore afraid that considerable damage may be sustained before the monster arrives in New York." The canoe arrived intact in 1883, having been shipped free of charge by the Panama Railroad Company and the Pacific Mail Company, and was immediately installed, suspended from the ceiling of the main hall. Since then, it has been the pride of succeeding generations of museum administrators. As the largest, best preserved, most beautifully made and painted canoe in any collection, it is one of the great monuments of Northwest Coast work, a symbol of the spectacular culture of these seafaring people.

It would be five years before another significant group of objects actually came into possession of the museum. In 1882, however, there appeared at Sitka, Alaska an individual whose name is associated with the largest number of Northwest Coast art objects that exist today, and who was the single most important contributor to the American Museum's Northwest Coast collections. Lieutenant George Thornton Emmons was born in 1852. He was one of three sons and a daughter of a naval officer, George Foster Emmons (1811-1884), who held a number of commands and positions and achieved the rank of Rear Admiral at the time of his retirement. The senior Emmons spent considerable time on duty on the West and Northwest coasts, and took part in the Wilkes Expedition to survey and explore parts of the Pacific and the west coast of Canada between 1838 and 1841. He was in command of one of the expedition's ships, the sloop *Peacock*, which was wrecked at the mouth of the Columbia River, shortly after the completion of the survey. The ethnographic material collected by G.F. Emmons and others from the Wilkes Expedition went to the Smithsonian and is some of the earliest from the Northwest Coast to have entered an American museum. Following this period, he came into command of numerous survey ships working along the American west coast and had many interesting contacts with the Indians of the area. During the time of the Alaska purchase (1866-1868), G.F. Emmons carried certain American commissioners there. His *New York Times* obituary states that he "hoisted the flag over that newly acquired teritory" at Sitka in 1868. It is said that he had a collection of ethnographic material in his Princeton home, and it is certain that he had considerable influence over the career and interests of his son.

The Rear Admiral was still alive when G.T. Emmons arrived at Sitka in 1882 and began to collect objects from the Tlingit. Only 30 then, he was to maintain his interest and enthusiasm for the material practically to the year of his death at the age of 93 in 1945. Although he was only interested in pieces that were no longer in use, and would never collect an object that still had meaning and significance to its owner, nothing would prevent Emmons from securing a piece he had decided to acquire. Some of the most significant objects he collected were from shamans' grave houses located on sites avoided by the Indians themselves. Many of the notes that Emmons made on the use and significance of these pieces provide invaluable documentation concerning the practice of shamanism on the Northwest Coast and often identify the specific spirit associated with a mask or other piece of equipment. Since much of this material was unique to each shaman, such detailed information is rarely documented. Emmons's enthusiasm for ferreting out objects is reflected in a letter written by him to John Winser, secretary of the American Museum in 1899. "I have just come across a set of Indian Doctors' implements; it has quite a local reputation, and while I have known of these things for years, I have never before been able to see them. . . . No white man has as yet seen them, and I have, I think arranged to keep them out of sight for a time until I hear if Mr. Jesup would wish them. The cost of the set is fifty-four dollars." (The group was purchased, and one piece from it is shown here, cat. no. 8.)

Interested in the history and meaning of each piece he collected, Emmons gathered as much information as he could about use and iconography, as well as any legends and myths that might be associated with them. Much of this was included in the handwritten notebooks he put together to describe the objects he sold to various museums. Some of his early photographs document the houses and monuments of the Tlingit, and he wrote a number of scholarly and popular articles on the subject of Indian culture and art.

There is not a major museum collection of Northwest Coast art in the United States without a significant body of material collected by Emmons. His pieces can be found in the Washington State Museum, The Denver Art Museum, the Field Museum of Natural History, the Smithsonian Institution, the Museum of the American Indian, the Portland Art Museum, the University Museum, Pennsylvania and the Buffalo Museum of Science. In addition, some parts of his collections found their way by exchange or purchase to the Provincial Museum, Victoria, the Otago Museum in Dunedin, the National Museum of Victoria in Melbourne and the Museum of Natural History and Ethnology in Dresden. But of all of these, it was the American Museum of Natural History that benefited the most from its association with Emmons. It owns about 5,200 objects collected by him; many are among the finest specimens of their kind. It is no accident that out of the 100 pieces represented in this exhibition, 61 are from Emmons.

The first group of objects collected by Emmons consists of 1,351 pieces he obtained in and around Sitka between 1882 and 1887. The majority of them are Tlingit, but some Haida and Bella Bella sculptures are included as well. The collection was purchased by the museum in 1888 for $12,000. In order to raise the funds for this acquisition, the trustees all contributed various amounts, and then passed the hat among friends and associates in New York, including Collis P. Huntington, Cornelius Vanderbilt, John D. Rockefeller and John Pierpont Morgan. The significance of this collection was duly noted in the Annual Report of 1888 which ends with a nice bit of prophesy that is particularly appropriate to this exhibition and catalogue:

> First in extent and importance is the collection gathered during five years residence in Alaska by Lieutenant G.T. Emmons, who enjoyed remarkable opportunities for gaining the confidence and helpful cooperation of the natives in obtaining the rare and frequently unique handiwork of their ancestors.... Each specimen was obtained by the Lieutenant himself, who kept a full record regarding it, and from such authentic data, he has prepared an elaborate catalogue, with full notes on the use made by the natives of each kind of object ... the series is ... probably more complete and authentic than any similar collection ever made in that portion of our continent ... the specimens of ancient times have already become exceedingly rare, and few more will ever be found. It is, therefore, gratifying to know that the workmanship of the aborigines of that land will be safely preserved for the benefit of investigators for all time.

The collection was placed on exhibition during the year. Between the Bishop material and this first Emmons collection the American Museum already had a very important group of over 2,100 pieces of Northwest Coast art. Nonetheless, much more was to come.

During the next few years, Emmons apparently continued his activities at the same pace and with the same extraordinary results. He put together a large collection for display at the World's Columbian Exposition in Chicago in 1893. After the close of the Fair, maintaining his loyalty to the American Museum, he sent it to New York for consideration for purchase. Turning to the Annual Report of 1893, we read, "The second collection gathered together by Lieutenant George T. Emmons, U.S. Navy, and which was incorporated in the Federal Government's Exhibit at Chicago has been brought to the museum for temporary display and inspection by our friends, and it is hoped that the museum may acquire it. It contains a much wider range of objects than the first collections purchased by the museum in 1888." It was announced in the following year that the museum had been able to purchase this collection agreeing to pay a stipulated amount over the next five

The Haida village of Skidegate, Queen Charlotte Island. Photograph, Edward Dossetter, 1881.

years. The total cost was just under $30,000 for 3,067 objects of similar age, quality and origin to those purchased six years before. These two accessions form the bulk of the Emmons collection at the museum, but the records show consistent involvement with him from 1896 to 1938. He never surrendered his interest in this material.

Throughout his long lifetime, the Lieutenant remained resolutely loyal to museums and looked with disdain on curio hunters, tourists and private collectors. His feelings are occasionally revealed in his letters. In 1898, for example, the museum had on approval from Emmons a group of 68 Tlingit objects, mostly pipes. It was apparently decided not to purchase the entire lot. In distress, he wrote from the ship *Minneapolis* to Franz Boas, ''. . . it seems a great pity that such valuable specimens should be lost, for I cannot give them away, neither can I keep them excepting a couple myself, and I shall send them back to Alaska, to be disposed of to tourists, who will, as you know, pay anything for such pieces. And they will be scattered about where they have no scientific value, and each one of them is a good article ethnologically considered.'' Fortunately, he prevailed and all 68 pieces were purchased.

The last major collection to be acquired from Emmons by the museum was a group of 352 sculptures from the Tsimshian that he had acquired in and around Kitikshan on the Upper Skeena River in 1909. By then he had clearly become aware that the heyday of Northwest Coast collecting was over. Writing from Prince Rupert in May 1910 at the time

he offered the material to the museum, he said, ''there are buyers for different museums and private collectors all along the coast, and old material is getting more difficult to procure each year.'' Emmons would have been pleased to see the memorandum that came down from curator Clark Wissler to President Henry Osborne on October 14, 1910, urging acquisition of the Tsimshian collection for a price of $2,300. He wrote, ''I may say that Lieutenant Emmons is one of our best collectors and does his work with a thoroughness that may well be envied by many who profess to be anthropologists.'' Two objects from this collection are the eagle mask, cat. no. 13 and the fine old storage box, cat. no. 72.

Much as had already been accomplished, there still remained some substantial collecting to be done to bring the Museum's Northwest Coast holdings to the strength they have today. The great depth of the Emmons and Bishop collections is in the art of the northern groups, particularly that of the Tlingit, Haida and Tsimshian peoples. There are some pieces of Bella Coola and Bella Bella origin, but material from the Kwakiutl was rare and that from such southern groups as the Nootka, Salish and Makah Indians was not included at all.

Once again, the museum was fortunate in having a talented curator and an interested, generous benefactor who came together to fill this gap. Franz Boas joined the staff of the museum as assistant curator of the Ethnological Division in 1895. He had previously worked under Adolf Bastian at the Royal Ethnological Museum in Berlin and was at the

The constant flow of movement, broken at rhythmic intervals by rather sudden, but not necessarily jerky changes of motion-direction, characterizes both the dance and art of the Northwest Coast.

BILL HOLM / 1965

museum when the great Kwakiutl collection gathered by Captain Adrian Jacobsen was received. He helped to catalogue it and the material, its documentation and Boas's field work formed the basis for his classic study, *The Social Organization of Secret Societies of the Kwakiutl Indians*, which was published in 1897. On his arrival in New York, Boas immediately set about to install and work with the riches gathered by Emmons and Powell. Immediately recognizing the lack of a proper representation from the Kwakiutl and other southern styles, he called this deficiency to the attention of the museum's president, Morris K. Jesup.

Jesup was one of the most generous and important men involved with the American Museum during its early years. He was among the original incorporators of the museum in 1868 and was a charter member of the board of trustees from the time of the founding of the museum the next year. In 1881 he was named president, a position he held until his death in 1908. Although the records show numerous contributions from him to the museum over the years, it was to the Jesup North Pacific Expedition that he made his deepest and most substantial commitment. The expedition was the idea of Franz Boas. As it says in the first volume of the Jesup Expedition series in which some of the results were published in 1905, its purpose was to investigate "the tribes, present and past on the coasts of the North Pacific Ocean, beginning on the Amoor River in Asia, extending northeastward to the Bering Sea, thence southeastward along the American coast as far as the Columbia River." Studies were to be made of social organization, language, religion, history, migration and exchange with particular emphasis on influence between east and west. Collections were, of course, to be formed as well. As expeditions go, this was comparatively informal and loosely organized. Nonetheless its results were spectacular, and by the time field work was completed in 1902 most of the gaps that Boas had seen in the collection were filled.

The busiest years of the expedition were 1897 and 1898. With a grant of $16,240 from Jesup, a number of well-known and highly regarded anthropologists were then able to visit various parts of the Northwest Coast to conduct studies in archaeology, linguistics and anthropology. James Teit and Harlan Smith worked among the Thompson Indians, Livingston Farrand studied the Salish and Fillip Jacobsen (the brother of Captain Adrian Jacobsen) collected from the Nootka and studied their ceremonies. Although all of these groups fall outside the limits set for this exhibition, the material they collected is an important part of the American Museum's holdings and has given it one of the best representations of the art and ethnography of the southern peoples. It was through these Jesup investigations, for example that the Jacobsen collection of Nootka masks and the Nootka whale house (acquired by George Hunt) ultimately came to the museum. Another aspect of the expedition, the investigation of the peoples of Siberia, was also carried out over the next several years. Berthold Laufer worked along the Amur River while Waldemar Jochelson and Waldemar Bogoras investigated the Chuckchee, Koryak and Yukageer tribes. All of them formed collections and studied cultural traits with specific attention to those that might have been shared on both sides of the Pacific.

In the context of this exhibition, it was the work of Franz Boas and George Hunt among the Kwakiutl that was of the greatest importance. In 1897, Boas returned to the Northwest Coast as a member of the Jesup Expedition to work with the Bella Coola and the Kwakiutl. He had met George Hunt during his earlier investigations for the Royal Ethnological Museum and had employed him as an interpreter. Hunt was part Kwakiutl and had assisted in collecting objects from his people for the World's Columbian Exposition in 1893; all of these are now in the Field Museum of Natural History. Boas had worked among the Kwakiutl as recently as 1895, recording myths and observing winter ceremonials and he immediately reestablished his relationship with Hunt. From 1897 to 1902, Hunt, who lived in Fort Rupert, became Boas's man in the field. Hunt was paid a salary to collect objects and to accompany Boas when he was in the area. He also agreed to collect myths and legends which he then transcribed in letters to Boas. For this he was paid fifty cents a page, the funds again contributed by Jesup. Hunt's knowledge of the language, customs and the people themselves was an invaluable resource. It not only brought a fine collection to the museum, but also enabled Boas to complete a number of highly significant studies on Kwakiutl myths, ethnology and customs. Boas and Hunt even collaborated on the writing of two im-

The Haida village of Masset, Queen Charlotte Island.
Photograph, Edward Dossetter, 1881.

portant volumes that were to come out of the Jesup Expedition: *Kwakiutl Texts* and *The Ethnology of the Kwakiutl.*

The two men had a warm and friendly relationship which is reflected in the correspondence between them. Only once does Boas display a bit of pique, when in 1902 he wrote, ''The price that you had to pay for the *Dzonoqwa* dish [$62.50] is very high . . . and I do not think the purchase was a very good one.'' The piece in question is one of those huge feast dishes in the form of the reclining giantess *Tsonoquoa*, the wild woman of the woods. Hunt justified his extravagance by saying he had seen a Kwakiutl family, which owned a similar one, refuse as much as $100 from another collector that same year. Although the dish is presently in storage because of its size, Boas would not regret its purchase today. Only three or four others have survived from this period. (Some idea of the size and drama of such a dish is given by the large mask cat. no. 44 which at one time decorated the face of one of them).

A particularly interesting aspect of the Boas-Hunt correspondence is the way in which it reveals the curator's collecting methods and goals. On April 14, 1897, before he went on the expedition, Boas wrote the following instructions to his friend:

> Our museum, for which you are going to work this summer, has no collections whatever from the Kwakiutl, therefore, anything you obtain will be welcome, but I ask you to keep a very careful list of everything you are getting. . . . If you should collect any masks, I think it will be better to wait until we get a chance to go to one of the remoter villages where they still have some of the old masks. If, however there should happen to be any good ones in Fort Rupert, there is no objection to collecting these, only we must remember that we want to have the tales and songs belonging to all of them.
>
> It occurred to me that in laying out our work, it would be a very good plan to have the Indians clearly understand what we are about. For this purpose, I enclose a letter which I have written to the Kwakiutl tribe. You know, of course, best whether the form of the letter is just what is wanted, and if not, I will ask you to make such changes as you think best. I hope you will read this letter to them, translated, of course into Indian, and in doing so, you better invite them to a feast, for which I will pay when I see you. . . .

Part of the letter of which Boas speaks was found in the files, and indicates something of the curator's sensitivity to the tragic situation of the Indians and of his ability to communicate with them on their own terms:

> Friends, [he writes] I am Mr. Boas who is speaking to you. I am he whom you called Heiltsaqoalis. It is two winters since I have been with you, but I have thought of you often. You were very kind to me when I was with you . . . I am thinking . . . that it is difficult for you to show to the white men in Victoria that your feasts and your potlatches are good, and I have tried to show them that they are good. . . . I am trying to do the right thing. I am trying to show them that your ways are not bad ways . . . I am sorry to see how many of your children do not obey the old laws, how they walk the ways of the white man. The ways of the Indian were made differently from the ways of the white man at the beginning of the world, and it is

good that we remember the old ways . . . your young
men do not know the history of your people. . . . It is
not good that these stories are forgotten. . . .

Although the last part of this letter has been lost,
from this beginning we can imagine the tone and
message of the rest of it. Boas obviously explained the
importance of preserving the objects, myths and oral
traditions of the Kwakiutl, which the Indians knew
would soon disappear. Whether Hunt ever read this
letter to the Kwakiutl is not known, but both Boas
and his friend maintained extremely good relationships with the Indians, and over the next five years
were able to gather a tremendous amount of information and a fine collection. The majority of the objects
of Kwakiutl origin shown here came to the museum
as a result of the collaboration between these two
men and the sponsorship of Jesup.

Boas was not quite as fortunate with Charles F.
Newcombe, a doctor in Victoria and a well-known
collector who accepted commissions from various
museums to gather objects in the field from Indian
families. Boas knew Newcombe from his previous
visits to the coast, and in 1900 wrote to ask him if he
would consider working for the museum. Boas was
hoping to have him become associated with John R.
Swanton, who was to be on Queen Charlotte Island
as part of the Jesup Expedition from September of that
year until the following August. Swanton made ex-
tensive collections from the Haida, including a
number of totem poles, masks and ethnographical
specimens, and the results of his year's stay would
appear in 1905 in a basic reference, *The Haida of*

Queen Charlotte Island, published as part of the
Jesup series. Newcombe actually did make a trip to
Queen Charlotte Island in 1901 for the American
Museum, and procured several important monumen-
tal carvings including some totem poles and the
Skedans coffin, cat. no. 70, but this was the only
significant group of objects to come there from him.

Competition from Chicago was the problem. At
the same time Boas had contacted Newcombe,
George A. Dorsey, a curator of Chicago's Field
Museum, also wrote, and offered the doctor a three
year contract to collect for his museum. Only able to
retain Newcombe for two months, Boas became
upset when certain objects he wanted for his
museum were acquired for Chicago instead. Refer-
ring to a stone figure he knew, he wrote to Newcombe in January, 1902, "I am very sorry you did not
get it for us rather than for the Field Columbian
Museum. I saw it in Chicago a few days ago. It is a
very good specimen." Newcombe's reply was
straightforward. He was working for Dorsey, and
would have to ask his permission before he could do
any additional collecting for Boas. The matter ended
when Boas wrote back, ". . . whatever specimens you
would pick up . . . illustrating the industrial side of
[Haida] life would be of particular value, and I should,
of course, want to have them at this Museum here.
For this reason, I do not believe that a combination of
work for Dorsey and for this Museum would be feasi-
ble." Newcombe subsequently put together some
fine collections for Chicago and a number of other
museums, but could not be brought back into as-

sociation with the American Museum.

Disappointed as Boas may have been, it was only a minor setback compared to the overall success of the Jesup project. With the completion of field work in 1902, it was announced in the Annual Report for that year, "The aim of the expedition . . . has been accomplished, and it now remains to study the relationship of these tribes by a detailed comparison of the material collected." By then, Jesup had contributed a total of about $60,000 to the costs of travel, acquisiton and shipping. For the next several years, the museum issued a number of publications in the Jesup Expedition series which brought the great value of the work to light. Although the detailed studies of cross-Pacific relationships between Siberia and the Northwest Coast were never written, the information and material gathered by those who took part in the Jesup Expedition has provided scholars of more recent times with the basic elements for their own research along these lines. Morris Jesup could well look with satisfaction on the results of his generous contribution.

The Bishop, Emmons and Jesup collections form about 90 percent of the Northwest Coast material in the American Museum. The remainder of the collection came to the museum through many different sources over a long period. A few of the more significant and interesting accessions are listed here:

1892 The museum purchases the entire James Terry collection, formed between 1867-91, consisting of 26,000 objects. Most of it is archaeological material from Southern California, the Mississippi Valley and the Columbia River Valley. Among the Northwest Coast pieces are Chilkat blankets, fine spoons, and a few shamans' ivories. Cat.no.65 is one of these.

1896 A collection of 176 objects is purchased for $835 from a Victoria dealer, S. Kirschberg. It had been on its way to New York to be sold at higher prices, but the steamer on which it was shipped burned and the cargo was sold for salvage. Included were four totem poles, masks, slate carvings and ethnographic items. The Haida slate, cat. no. 98, is one of these.

1904 An Alaskan collection is transferred to the museum from the Bronx Zoological Park. Among 73 objects, mostly Tlingit, were masks, boxes, bowls and halibut hooks. Although there is reference to a Harriman Expedition as the source of this collection, details are not known.

1905 Adolph Lewisohn gives the museum a collection of 180 objects that was formed by Lewis Levy of Juneau. It is mostly Tlingit and includes baskets, masks, rattles and a shaman's box complete with its contents.

1905 Mrs. Albert Bierstadt, widow of the Hudson River School painter, gives 24 American Indian objects from her husband's collection to the museum. The Haida ladle, cat. no. 90, was among them.

1909 Six Haida and Bella Bella houseposts and totem poles collected by Harlan Smith arrive. They were purchased at the going rate of $1.00 per foot plus shipment.

1910 John Pierpont Morgan purchases Emil Lander's collection of Tlingit and Haida spoons and gives it to the museum.

1912 A collection of 177 sculptures, mostly from the Tlingit and Kwakiutl, formed by a "Governor Brady" (probably John C. Brady) is purchased for the museum by Mrs. Edward H. Harriman. The Tlingit shaman's mask, cat. no. 9, was among them.

1930 Mary Hall Sayre gives a group of 16 Tlingit pieces in memory of her brother, Reginald Sayre, among which was the rattle, cat. no. 56, and the halibut hook, cat. no. 95.

1939 115 Haida pieces collected by Paul Wander in about 1930 on Queen Charlotte Island are given by Miss Ruth Anderson.

1946 Mrs. J. Marvin Wright presents the Mac-Murray Indian Collection to the museum. It consists of 156 objects and was formed by her mother and father between about 1870 and 1910. Included were Tlingit and Haida pieces some of which were purchased from Emmons in Alaska. A spoon, cat. no. 85, was from this collection.

1963 53 baskets, mostly Tlingit are given by the Melgina Chapter of the National Society of the Daughters of the American Revolution. The collection was formed between 1906-08 by Augusta Alexander Greene when her husband was stationed at Fort Seward.

After the 1930's, fewer and fewer pieces were given to the American Museum. Most of the important early material that survived had been collected by museums, and relatively little Northwest Coast art was still privately owned. Furthermore, it is not likely that many pieces of great significance will be given or purchased in the future. Over the last few years, private collectors and some Canadian museums have been buying good Northwest Coast art that happens to come on the market and paying very high prices for it. Compared to the present day value of Northwest Coast art, the sums paid for the purchase of the Bishop collection, the two large Emmons collections and the amount of the entire Jesup grant seems tiny.

Certainly these were different times, and it is important to place such facts in their proper context. Whatever these amounts signify to us today, they represented a substantial commitment on the part of the museum at the time. Information provided by the Chase Manhattan Bank shows that today's dollar would have had the purchasing power of 13 cents in 1900. Conversely, a 1900 dollar is valued at $7.26 in 1978. The American Museum spent a total of about 120,000 of these dollars on the Bishop, Emmons and Jesup collections. At this time, the annual budget of the entire museum was in the neighborhood of $300,000, and it is certain that the funds allocated to the acquisition of the Northwest Coast collections represented a large proportion of those that were available to the Ethnology Department as a whole.

It must also be remembered that these pieces were not being collected as art, but, as "ethnological specimens," and they were priced accordingly, despite the growing interest in them that was being shown by museums. The records suggest that the col-

Tsimshian totem poles at Kitwanga. Photograph,
Canadian News Service, c. 1930.

dependently wealthy and well paid by the Navy, so
would not have sought to make much money on
these transactions. These early collectors were will-
ing to advance their own funds to acquire objects for
museum collections. None of them ever became
wealthy dealing in Northwest Coast art.

Interesting as the financial details may be, the
quality of the objects and the scope of the collection
is of far greater importance. There are only a few
other collections that compare to this one, and all of
them were formed at the same time. These are those
at the Smithsonian Institution, Washington; the
Field Museum of Natural History, Chicago; the National Museum of Man, Ottawa; and the Museum of
the American Indian, New York. Although there are
also important collections at the Royal Ontario
Museum in Toronto; the University of British Columbia, Vancouver, and the Provincial Museum in
Victoria, they do not have as broad a representation
or the quantity of objects owned by these other
museums. The great value of the American Museum
holdings is not only in its depth but in the collection
data that was gathered and has been preserved, and
the fact that much of the material was studied and
published at a time when the Indian cultures were
still living. Because of the early support of such men
as Heber Bishop and Morris Jesup, the research and
dedication of scholars like Franz Boas, John Swanton
and Harlan Smith, and the commitment of such
early collectors as Israel W. Powell, George Hunt and
above all, George T. Emmons, this collection is probably the best of them all.

lectors asked sums that were the same or only
slightly higher than those they had originally paid.
Newcombe and Hunt were given a salary to collect
and passed on the pieces they purchased at the same
prices. Powell seems only to have been reimbursed
for his purchases, and Emmons was both in-

Every minor feature of Northwest Coast style contributes to one basic quality: its strength and self-assertive vitality . . . few cultures have so consistently developed these traits while combining them with a marked sensitivity to nuances of form and the highest standards of craftsmanship.

ERNA GUNTHER / 1966

Catalogue of the Exhibition

Masks

Of all Northwest Coast artistic creations, masks have the greatest sculptural variety. They were worn at such social ceremonies as feasts and potlatches, at winter initiation ceremonies, and during magic and curing rituals performed by shamans. Often the exact significance of a mask has been lost because such information was only known by those who owned and used them.

In the north, among the Tlingit, Tsimshian and Haida, masks were most often used at feasts and potlatches. The head of a family would wear the specific mask that represented the crest animal of his clan while he acted as a host, delivered speeches and lead and observed the dances that were held to reenact the myths of his family. Dancers who participated in these performances were also furnished with masks that corresponded to the roles they played. These masks could be in the form of a simple face covering, a visor which was worn on the forehead, a helmet which completely covered the head, or a hat. They were carved to represent a wide variety of animals including birds, fish, land and sea mammals, insects and supernatural spirits. Certain old helmets carved in the form of human faces were actually portraits of specific chiefs. Originally made to be worn during warfare, in more recent times they also came to be used at ceremonies. Helmets and masks worn by the family head were the most valued heirlooms of the clan.

Closely allied in use and significance are the headdress frontlets. These are rectangular, oval, or round convex carvings that were attached to elaborate headdresses. They were worn by high ranking people to emphasize their status and position, and carved to represent legends, totemic crests, or episodes in a particular clan's history.

In the south, masks were worn for similar purposes, but among the Kwakiutl, other forms of spectacular masks were made for use during the winter initiation ceremonies held by the Cannibal Society. These masks represent fantastic bird monsters and supernatural beings associated with the man-eating spirit. They are often of large size and made with moveable parts activated by pulling strings so that mouths and eyes can be made to open and close. Fins and flippers of sea monster masks would be moved to imitate swimming motions. Cannibal Society masks take the form of visors, face coverings, or helmets. It was in the south that the transformation mask reached its highest development. Such masks were constructed so that the outer mask face could be opened up to reveal the carvings of another individual or spirit inside.

Throughout the entire Northwest Coast, masks were also extensively used by shamans in connection with healing, divination and magic performances. Shamans' masks are usually in the form of simple face coverings worn by the shaman or his helper. They represented the spirits that the shaman called upon to aid him in each particular ritual, and thus provided tangible evidence of the shaman's power and alliances. Each shaman possessed his own personal set of masks.

Miniature masks were also part of a shaman's paraphernalia. Often a performing shaman would wear a headdress made of down feathers, spruce roots, cedar bark and a variety of other materials to which the miniature mask was attached. Such maskettes represented the aiding spirit. Other miniature masks might be sewn on to shamans' aprons, and served similar functions. Often these small masks were kept unattached and affixed to a specific headdress or apron as they were needed.

**SHAMAN'S FACE MASK,
TLINGIT**
**wood, traces of black and blue
pigment, 21.6 cm. h.**

*Collected by G. T. Emmons
between 1884-93 from a
shaman's grave house on the
Akwe River. The mask was the
property of a shaman named
Setan and represents the spirit
of a dead man with a protruding
tongue. Collected with cat. nos.
3, 4 and 52.*

2

3.
**SHAMAN'S FACE MASK,
TLINGIT**
**wood, operculum, traces of red,
blue and black pigment,
22.5 cm. h.**

*Collected by G. T. Emmons
with cat. nos. 2, 4 and 52.
Emmons's notes state that it
represents "the spirit of a
drowned man turning into a
land otter man."*

4.
**SHAMAN'S FACE MASK,
TLINGIT**
**wood, fiber, traces of blue, red,
white and black pigment,
18.5 cm. h.**

*Collected by G. T. Emmons
with cat. nos. 2, 3 and 52.
According to Emmons's notes,
the mask represents "a good
natured spirit who lives in the air."*

3

**SHAMAN'S FACE MASK,
TLINGIT**
**wood, black, green and red
pigment, 23.6 cm. h.**

*Collected by G. T. Emmons
between 1882-87 from a
shaman's grave house near
Chilkat. The mask represents a
spirit known for its loud voice
and the ability to hear over long
distances. The attributes are indicated by the protruding lips
and the two pairs of ears.*

5

6.
**SHAMAN'S FACE MASK,
TLINGIT**
**wood, bear skin, rawhide,
white, blue, red and black
pigment, 20.5 cm. h. (exclusive
of hair)**

*Collected by G. T. Emmons
between 1884-93 from a
shaman's grave house at Dry
Bay. Emmons gives the Tlingit
name of this spirit as Kush-tar-
kah. A land otter man is
represented. Collected with
cat. no. 7.*

7.
**SHAMAN'S FACE MASK,
TLINGIT**
**wood, rawhide, black, white,
red and traces of blue pigment,
21.1 cm. h.**

*Collected by G. T. Emmons
with cat. no. 6. Emmons identifies it as representing the spirit
of a chiton, but it seems to suggest the features of an old man.*

6

7

**8.
SHAMAN'S FACE MASK,
TLINGIT**
wood, rawhide, black, blue and
red pigment, 23.4 cm. h.

*Collected by G. T. Emmons
from a grave house at Berner's
Bay. The mask was the property
of a shaman named Kowee who
was said to have died 40 or 50
years before the mask was collected. It probably represents
the spirit of a devilfish as a row
of tentacles can be seen encir-
cling the face.*

**9.
SHAMAN'S FACE MASK,
TLINGIT**
wood, rawhide, red, black and
blue pigment, 20.8 cm. h.

*Gift of Mrs. Edward H. Har-
riman in 1912. Purchased from
the Governor Brady (probably
John C. Brady) collection. An
old label on the back of the
mask reads, "Doctor dancing
mask representing a Nass River
Indian."*

**10.
SHAMAN'S FACE MASK,
TLINGIT**
wood, black, red, blue and
traces of white pigment,
22.3 cm. h.

*Collected by G. T. Emmons
between 1884-93 from a grave
house on the Ankau-Lost River
drainage, twenty miles south-
east of Yakutat. An eagle spirit
is represented.*

8

9

10

11.
SHAMAN'S FACE MASK,
TLINGIT
wood, rawhide, animal skin,
operculum, blue and red
pigment, 21.0 cm. h.

Collected by G. T. Emmons
between 1882-87 at Chilkat. An
old man is represented.

12.
SHAMAN'S FACE MASK,
TLINGIT
wood, operculum, ivory, hair,
animal skin, rawhide, red,
white and green pigment, 20.0
cm. h. (exclusive of hair)

Collected by G. T. Emmons
between 1882-87 at Chilkat. A
dead man is represented.

12

13.
FACE MASK, TSIMSHIAN
wood, animal skin, rawhide,
white, red and black pigment,
20.4 cm. h.

Collected by G. T. Emmons in
1909 at Kitikshan, Upper
Skeena River. The eyes are
moveable, appearing white
when closed and red when
opened. An eagle is represented.

13

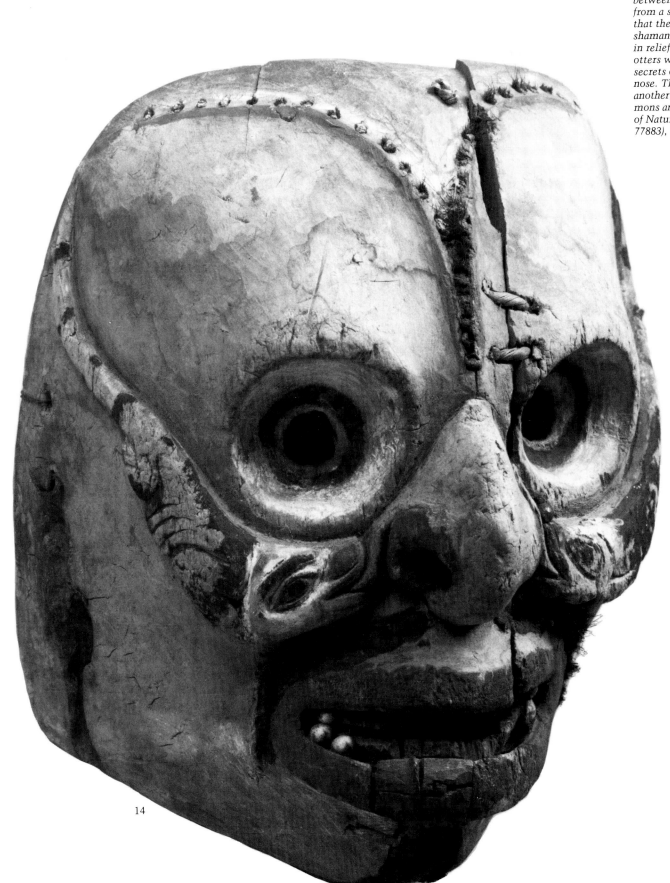

14.
**SHAMAN'S FACE MASK,
TLINGIT**
**wood, operculum, rawhide,
spruce root, twine, hair, red and
white pigment, 20.5 cm. h.**

*Collected by G. T. Emmons
between 1882-87 at Chilkat
from a shaman. Emmons states
that the mask represents a dead
shaman. The two figures carved
in relief below the eyes are land
otters which are extracting the
secrets of the shaman from his
nose. This mask is similar to
another, also collected by Emmons and in the Field Museum
of Natural History, Chicago, (no.
77883), see Maurer, E. no. 493.*

14

15. CHIEF'S HEADDRESS, TLINGIT
 copper, hair, velvet, rawhide, 14.8 cm. h.

Collected by G. T. Emmons between 1884-93 "from Kehk country." Emmons's notes state that this headdress was part of a chief's ceremonial costume and was worn for fighting. He interprets the incised design as representing a sea lion.

**16.
FOREHEAD MASK, TLINGIT**
 wood, blanket cloth, haliotis, hair, metal, rawhide, white, red and blue pigment, 17.0 cm. h.

Collected by G. T. Emmons between 1882-87 at Sitka. A bear is represented.

17.
VISOR MASK, TLINGIT
wood, operculum, animal teeth,
red, black and traces of green
pigment, 23.5 cm. l.

*Collected by G. T. Emmons be-
tween 1884-93. A wolf head is
represented. The right ear, paw
and most of the teeth are
restored.*

18.
**SHAMAN'S HELMET,
TLINGIT**
wood, twine, copper, animal
skin, rawhide, blue, black and
red pigment, 27.5 cm. l.

*Collected by G. T. Emmons be-
tween 1884-93 near Angoon.
Emmons identifies the bird as a
kingfisher. The bottom figure is
a frog.*

17

19

19.
SHAMAN'S HEADDRESS MASK, TLINGIT
wood, black, red and traces of white pigment, 14.7 cm. h.

Collected by G. T. Emmons between 1882-87 from a grave house at Hootznahoo near Port Frederick. Emmons's notes identify the figure as a wolf spirit, though it seems more likely that a bear is represented. Two human faces are carved on the ears.

20.
SHAMAN'S HEADDRESS, TLINGIT
wood, bear fur, ermine fur, ivory, haliotis, red, green and black pigment, 12.4 cm. h. (mask only)

Collected by G. T. Emmons between 1882-87 at Chilkat. According to Emmons, the headdress was worn by a shaman during ceremonies to heal wounds. The protruding tongue was touched to the afflicted area. The walrus ivory charm attached to the framework is carved in the form of a land otter.

21.
SHAMAN'S HEADDRESS, TLINGIT
wood, brass, operculum, haliotis, animal hide, feathers, hair, down, caribou tail, red, black and blue pigment, 14.0 cm. h. (mask only)

Collected by G. T. Emmons between 1884-93 at Klukwan.

20

21

**22.
SHAMAN'S HEADDRESS
MASK, TLINGIT**
wood, hair, haliotis, red and
traces of green pigment,
17.2 cm. h.

*Collected by G. T. Emmons
between 1882-87 at Chilkat.
Emmons states that the mask
represents a devilfish and it was
worn by a shaman when he was
in enmity with other shamans.
The eyebrows are in the form of
tentacles.*

**23.
SHAMAN'S HEADDRESS
MASK, TSIMSHIAN**
wood, red, black and blue
pigment, 10.7 cm. l.

*Collected by I. W. Powell in
1881, H. R. Bishop Collection.
A raven is represented.*

23

FACE MASK, HAIDA
wood, cloth strips, red, black
and blue pigment, 27.6 cm. h.

*Collected by G. T. Emmons be-
tween 1882-87 from Howkan.
Emmons's notes state that the
mask represents "a man and an
owl talking."*

24

25.
FACE MASK, BELLA BELLA
wood, animal skin, nails,
haliotis, white, black, red and
blue pigment, 25.5 cm. h.

Collected by I. W. Powell in
1881, H. R. Bishop Collection.
According to Boas, a spirit of
the moon is represented. Swan-
ton, however, interprets it as
signifying cumulus clouds, ''the
clouds being indicated by white
triangular marks.''

26.
VISOR MASK, HAIDA
wood, rawhide, twine, nails, white, red, black and blue pigment, 63.7 cm. l.

Collected by G. T. Emmons between 1884-93 on Prince of Wales Island. A crane is represented.

27.
VISOR MASK, KWAKIUTL, HAMATSA SOCIETY
wood, twine, cedar bark, feathers, white, blue, red and black pigment, 93.0 cm. l. (mask only)

Collected by G. Hunt in 1899 at Fort Rupert. This type of mask represents a bird monster known to the Kwakiutl as hokhokw. It was believed to crack men's skulls open and eat the brain. The masks were worn in Hamatsa Society dances and were associates of the man eating spirit.

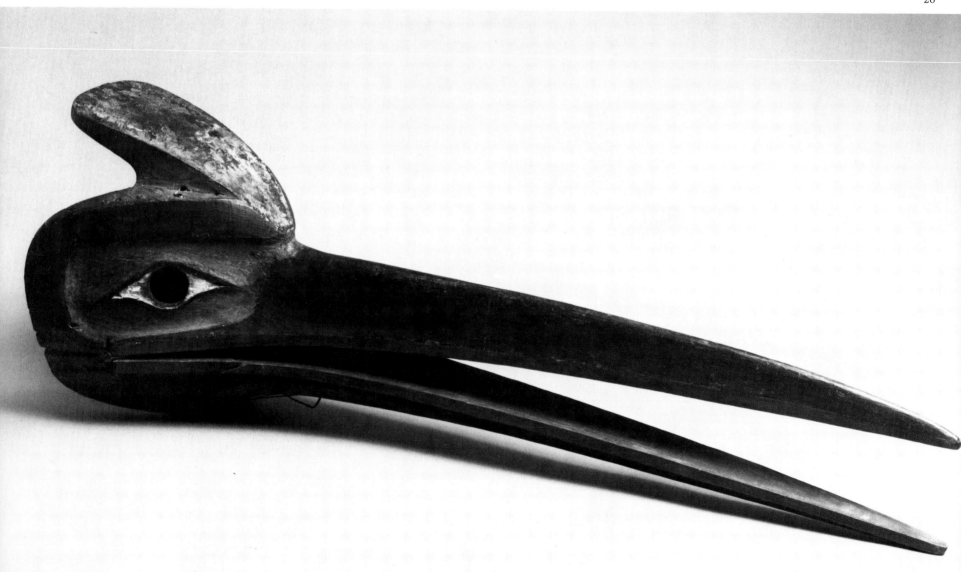

28.
**HEAD FROM A GRAVE
MONUMENT, KWAKIUTL**
wood, traces of red and black
pigment, 141.0 cm. l.

*Collected by F. Boas in 1894 at
Fort Rupert. This head is part of
the figure of a standing bird that
was originally made as a grave
monument for a Kwakiutl chief.
The rest of the figure is in the
collection, but was too fragile
to include in the exhibition.
Boas identifies the bird as
representing the crane-like
monster Hokhokw which
became a clan emblem among
the Kwakiutl, and was an important character in the
Hamatsa Society dances (cat. no.27).*

28

27

29.
VISOR MASK, BELLA BELLA, HAMATSA SOCIETY
wood, twine, bear skin, white, black and red pigment, 50.3 cm. l.

Collected by F. Boas in 1894 from the Bella Bella. This is another version of a crooked beak mask. There is a painting of an animal head on the lower jaw which may represent a sculpin.

30.
VISOR MASK, KWAKIUTL HAMATSA SOCIETY
wood, twine, nails, black, red, white and green pigment, 73.0 cm. l. (mask only)

Collected by G. Hunt in 1897 at Fort Rupert. Such masks are known as crooked beak masks and represent mythical birds. They were worn by men in dances for the Hamatsa during the taming of the initiates into the Society. The Kwakiutl name for the mask is galodwudzuwis.

31.
FACE MASK, HAIDA
wood, animal hide, nails, twine, white, blue, black and red pigment, 23.0 cm. h.

Collected by G. T. Emmons between 1884-93 on Prince of Wales Island. Two different aspects of a spirit, perhaps male and female, are shown by this transformation mask.

29

30

32.
CHIEF'S HEADDRESS, HAIDA
wood, wool, haliotis, cloth,
ermine pelts, sea lion whiskers,
red, blue and black pigment,
19.5 cm. h. (frontlet), 157.0 cm. h.
(approximate total height)

*Collected by G. T. Emmons be-
tween 1884-93. Emmons's
notes identify the top figure of
the frontlet as a bear and the
bottom one as a blackfish.
Although he collected this piece
from the Tlingit, he believed it
to have been made by the Haida.*

33.
**CHIEF'S HEADDRESS
ORNAMENT, TLINGIT**
wood, haliotis, red, blue and
black pigment, 18.3 cm. h.

*Collected by G. T. Emmons be-
tween 1884-93. A hawk is
represented.*

33

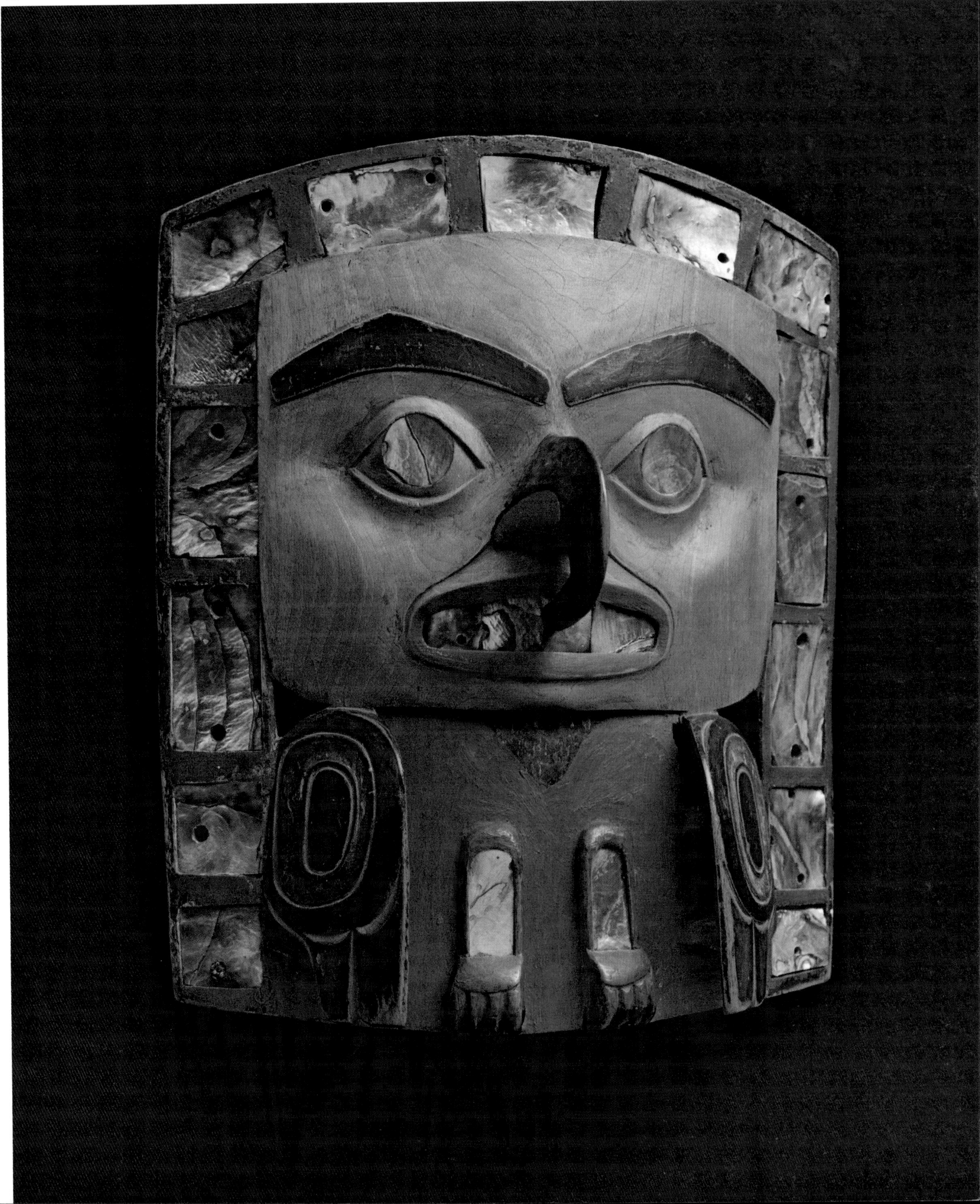

34.
SHAMAN'S HEADDRESS
MASK, TLINGIT
wood, teeth, animal skin,
black, blue and red pigment,
14.0 cm. l.

Collected by G. T. Emmons be-
tween 1882-87 from a shaman's
grave house. A wolf is
represented.

34

**35.
POTLATCH TRANSFORMA-
TION MASK, KWAKIUTL**
wood, twine, animal hide, blue,
red, green, white and black
pigment, 45.0 cm. h.
*Collected by G. Hunt in 1897 at
Fort Rupert. The mask was
worn at potlatches for the
Yaaixagame clan of which the
wolf was the ancestor. The
outer sculpture and the painting
on the inner surfaces of the
opened mask represent the
wolf. The bird head on the inside represents a raven.*

36.
**HELMET MASK, KWAKIUTL,
HAMATSA SOCIETY**
wood, black, red and green
pigment, 46.5 cm. h.

*Collected by F. Boas in 1896.
According to Boas, the mask
represents the powerful spirit of
a cannibal grizzly bear, known
to the Kwakiutl as bakbak-
walanooksiwae. The mask was
worn at the beginning of the
cannibal dance of the Hamatsa
Society.*

37.
VISOR MASK, BELLA BELLA
wood, twine, nails, red, blue
and black pigment, 66.2 cm. l.

Collected by F. Boas and G.
Hunt in 1897. A raven is
represented.

37

38.
VISOR MASK, KWAKIUTL
wood, traces of black pigment,
65.0 cm.

*Collected by G. Hunt in 1900 at
Koskimo Village, Vancouver
Island. The mask represents a
wolf and the small head carved
on the lower jaw is in the form
of a hawk.*

39.
HELMET, KWAKIUTL
wood, hair, red, black and white
pigment, 43.8 cm. l.

*Collected by G. Hunt in 1901.
Two wolf heads are represented.
Boas gives the Kwakiutl name
for this mask as yaxtal.*

40.
**VISOR MASK, KWAKIUTL,
HAMATSA SOCIETY**
wood, twine, metal, bear fur,
red, green, white, blue and
black pigment, 91.0 cm. l.

*Collected by G. Hunt in 1897 at
Fort Rupert. Such masks represent a grizzly bear spirit known
to the Kwakiutl as dluwalakha.
They were worn by dancers who
were dressed in a bear fur
costume. The dances were
comic in nature and took place
during lulls in the Hamatsa
Society ceremonies.*

38

39

41.
HEADDRESS, HAIDA
wood, animal skin, rawhide,
down, hair, twine, black and
red pigment, 71.0 cm. l.

Collected by I. W. Powell in
1881, H. R. Bishop collection.
Such articulated headdresses
were worn during dances for th
Olala Society and represent a
cannibal spirit.

42.
PUPPET HEAD, KWAKIUTL
wood, hair, rawhide, black and
white pigment, 18.4 cm. h.

Collection data for this piece is
missing, but it was most prob-
ably collected by F. Boas and/c
G. Hunt between 1896 and
1901. The head originally
belonged to a puppet figure, an
may have been used by a
shaman, or in ceremonies
related to those of the Olala
Society (see cat. no. 41).

43.
FACE MASK, BELLA COOLA
wood, red and black pigment,
28.4 cm. h.

*Collected by G. Hunt in 1897.
A thunderbird spirit is
represented.*

44.
**MASK FROM A FEAST DISH,
KWAKIUTL**
wood, bear skin, black, red and
traces of white pigment,
80.0 cm. h.

*Collected by G. Hunt in 1902.
Such masks were part of very
large feast dishes that are in the
shape of a reclining figure
representing* Tsonoquoa, *the
wild woman of the woods.*

43

45.
FACE MASK, BELLA COOLA
wood, cedar bark fibers,
feathers, metal staples, white,
blue, red and black pigment,
66.0 cm. h.

*Collected by F. Boas and G.
Hunt in 1897. Boas identifies
the mask as representing the
sun.*

46.
FACE MASK, BELLA COOLA
wood, blue, red and black
pigment, 38.0 cm. h.

*Collected by I. W. Powell in
1881, H. R. Bishop collection.
Boas's catalogue notes state
that the mask represents a
"whistling demon."*

46

47.
SHAMAN'S DANCE SHIRT, HAIDA
animal hide, quills, red and black pigment, 121.0 cm. l.
Collected by G. T. Emmons between 1884-93 at Howkan. Emmons identifies the two figures on each side as eagles. The human-like forms in the center of the shirt are identified by Emmons as spirits that live in the sky, and the large seated animal at the bottom center is a bear.

Textiles and Painted Hide Costumes

Although the Indians of the Northwest Coast did not cultivate fiber-producing plants or domesticate wool-producing animals, they were able to use materials at hand to produce fine textiles. The warp for these textiles was made of the inner bark of the cedar tree, finely shredded and twisted into a string-like form. This was then wrapped in mountain goat wool, and the weft was spun entirely of mountain goat wool.

Both men and women participated in the creation of textiles. Men hunted the goats, constructed the weaving frame, cut and prepared the necessary measuring sticks, and painted the pattern board from which the designs would be copied. Women then spun and dyed the yarn and did the actual weaving. Because the design shapes are frequently rounded and ovoid, the entire textile could not be woven all at once on a standard loom as such a technique could only produce angular forms. Each part of the design therefore had to be made separately and then embroidered together with the others to form the overall pattern. At least six months were required to complete one piece of weaving.

Chilkat blankets, so called from the name of a sub-group of the Tlingit people who specialized in their manufacture, are the best-known textiles of the Northwest Coast. They were widely traded, and were used throughout the northern area, worn as a shawl over the shoulders during important social occasions. Chilkat designs relate to family histories, but are extremely abstract. Even with specific information from the owners themselves, conflicting interpretations about the meaning of the various design elements are often encountered. Therefore, no attempts to decipher their meaning are made here.

Other textiles were made to be worn as chiefs' tunics, dance aprons, and leggings. Textiles were occasionally used for smaller objects such as hats and bags but these seem to be fragments salvaged from larger weavings.

Other ritual and ceremonial garments such as dance capes and tunics, shamans' aprons and leggings were made of animal hide. Caribou and deerskin was most commonly used and crest designs or motifs depicting supernatural beings were painted on the outer surface. These skin costumes are usually fringed and are often decorated with other materials including quills, blanket cloth strips, puffin beaks and deer hoofs.

48.
BLANKET, TLINGIT,
CHILKAT
mountain goat wool, cedar
bark, velvet and red cloth, blue,
yellow and black pigment,
156.0 cm. w. (top)

Collected by I. W. Powell in
1881, H. R. Bishop Collection.

49.
BLANKET, TLINGIT,
CHILKAT
mountain goat wool, cedar
bark, animal hide, black, yellow
and blue pigment, 152.0 cm. w.
(top)

Collected by I. W. Powell in
1881, H. R. Bishop Collection.

50.
RAVEN RATTLE, TLINGIT
wood, red, green and black
pigment, 31.5 cm. 1.
Collected by G. T. Emmons between 1882-87 at Sitka. A recumbent shaman lies on the back of the raven, his tongue extended to the mouth of a raven. The figure of a hawk with a frog on its mouth is carved on the bottom of the rattle.

Rattles
and Speakers' Staffs

Rattles were used to accompany dances and singing, and also to emphasize important points of oratory. Most are wood, but there are some examples made of mountain sheep horn and copper. The most common form, the raven rattle, was primarily used by chiefs or headmen during social ceremonies. Raven rattles are said to have originated among the Tsimshian, but by the end of the nineteenth century, the form was so widespread, it was used throughout the northern area. The body of these rattles consists of a raven, and the head of a hawk is carved on the breast. Usually a reclining male figure, probably representing a shaman, is carved on the back of the rattle. His tongue is joined to that of a frog or bird, a motif apparently representing the transference of power from one to another.

Other rattle types were used only by shamans, the most common being the so-called oyster catcher rattle which takes the shape of the long beaked shore bird. Various human and animal figures carved on the back of the rattle represent the shaman and his spirit assistants. The sound of the rattle indicated a supernatural presence.

Speakers' staffs, sometimes called talking sticks were used by chiefs or speakers when gifts were made, or during speeches. They were hit on the wood floor as the name of each recipient of a gift was announced, or to stress parts of oratory. Carvings on them represent family origin myths.

50

51.
SPEAKER'S STAFF,
KWAKIUTL
wood, 138.0 cm. l.

*Collected by I. W. Powell in
1881, H. R. Bishop Collection.
The lower figure has a land
otter on the back of the head.*

52.
RAVEN RATTLE, TLINGIT
wood, rawhide, traces of blue
and red pigment, 32.5 cm. l.

*Collected by G. T. Emmons
with cat. nos. 2, 3 and 4. The
fact that such an old, well used
raven rattle was found with the
paraphernalia of a shaman indicates that this form of rattle
was used by shamans as well as
chiefs.*

53.
RATTLE FRAGMENT, HAIDA
wood, red, black and green
pigment, 16.5 cm. h.

*Collected by G. T. Emmons
between 1884-93. Emmons's
notes read "one spirit within
another, both singing."
Although catalogued as a headdress ornament, Philip Gifford
has suggested that the carving
originally formed the front of a
large round rattle.*

54.
CHIEF'S RATTLE, TLINGIT
wood, black and red pigment,
30.5 cm. h.

*Collected by G. T. Emmons
before 1904 at Wrangell. The
rattle represents a human face
in the center of a bear paw.
Although Emmons believed this
rattle to be Haida, it is similar
in style and age to a well-known
example in the Washington
State Museum, (no. 955), which
was once the property of the
Tlingit chief Shakes.*

51

52

53

54

55

56

57

55.
SHAMAN'S RATTLE, TLINGIT
wood, spruce root fiber, wire,
down, red and black pigment,
30.7 cm. l.

*Collected by G. T. Emmons
between 1882-87 at Taku. The
body of the rattle is in the form
of an oyster catcher. The figure
of a reclining shaman lies on
the back of the bird with two
fish forms on each side. Emmons identifies the head next to
the handle as representing a
land otter.*

56.
SHAMAN'S RATTLE, TLINGIT
wood, rawhide, animal skin, red
and blue pigment, 30.1 cm. l.

*Gift to the Museum in 1930 by
Mary Sayre in memory of
Reginald Sayre. Two old labels
once affixed to the rattle provide the information that the
rattle was originally presented
by Captain Henriques to Dr.
Sterling who gave it to Louis A.
Sayre in 1875. The body is in
the form of an oyster catcher
with the figure of a frog carved
on the back.*

57.
SHAMAN'S RATTLE, TLINGIT
wood, twine, rawhide, black,
red and green pigment,
32.5 cm. l.

*Collected by G. T. Emmons
before 1904 at Angoon,
Admiralty Island. The three
figures carved on the back of
this oyster catcher rattle represent some shaman activity or
legend. Drucker has described
the scene as showing "a person
pursued by a wolf escaping on
the back of a sea monster,"
while Emmons states it
represents "an otter tying a
witch spirit with a rope of
twisted bark."*

58.
**SHAMAN'S HEADREST,
TLINGIT**
wood, black pigment,
51.8 cm. l.

*Collected by G. T. Emmons
between 1882-87 at Chilkat.
Emmons's notes state that the
heads "demonstrate the singing
and talking positions of the face
and mouth." Such headrests
were sometimes used during
fasts while the shaman was
engaged in a quest for a spirit.
Philip Gifford has pointed out
that the head of the reclining
shaman figure on the back of
the rattle, cat. no. 55, rests on
such an object.*

59

60

Shaman's Guardian Figures

Shamans relied on guardian figures to protect them from disease, evil spirits and the spells of other shamans or witches. Some are in human form and had specific powers, others, of a more generally protective nature, took the form of animals. The most powerful were made to protect the corpse of a shaman after he had been placed in his grave house.

59.
SHAMAN'S SPIRIT FIGURE,
TLINGIT
wood, hair, twine, red, blue and
black pigment, 23.5 cm. l.

Collected by G. T. Emmons
between 1882-87 at Shakaw.
Emmons's notes state that this
carving was held near a fire by a
shaman. When it was heated, it
was rubbed against the afflicted
part of a patient or left with him
in order to effect a cure.

60.
SHAMAN'S GUARDIAN
FIGURE, TLINGIT
wood, metal, operculum, black,
red and traces of green pigment,
33.5 cm. l.

Collected by G. T. Emmons
between 1882-87 at Chilkat.
Emmons states that this carv-
ing, which represents a sea
monster, was originally fasten-
ed over the door of a shaman's
dwelling to ward off sickness
and evil spirits.

61.
SHAMAN'S GUARDIAN
FIGURE, TLINGIT
wood, hair, eagle down, oper-
culum, red, green, black and
brown pigment, 59.8 cm. h.

Collected by G. T. Emmons be-
tween 1882-87 from a shaman's
grave at Yakutat. Emmons
describes this figure as a guar-
dian spirit which protected the
shaman's corpse from hostile
spirits. The human heads carv-
ed in the kneecaps and the wolf
head on the chest represent
spirits which serve the guar-
dian. The figure originally stood
on the back of a seal figure
which symbolized its ability to
travel as silently and easily as a
seal through water.

61

**62.
SHAMAN'S GUARDIAN
FIGURE, TLINGIT**
**wood, hair, abalone, black
pigment, 45.0 cm. h.**

*Collected by G. T. Emmons
between 1882-87 at Chilkat.
Emmons's notes state that the
figure was used to taste the
water a shaman was about to
drink to guard against spirits,
the evil doing of witches and
danger. The figure of a shark is
carved into the back.*

63.
STANDING FIGURE,
TLINGIT
wood, hair, bird bone, animal
hide, red and black pigment,
17.8 cm. h. (exclusive of hair)

Collected by G. T. Emmons be-
tween 1882-87 at Chilkat. The
figure represents a shaman.
Although Emmons suggests its
use as a child's doll, it is un-
doubtedly a shaman's ac-
cessory.

63

64.
SHAMAN'S CHARM, TLINGIT
ivory, 15.6 cm. l.

Collected by G. T. Emmons between 1882-87 from a shaman's grave house near Huna. This charm is one of a set of six that were originally attached to a shaman's animal skin dance apron. Emmons identifies the central figure as the spirit Kewar-klus which was believed to live "in a far distant country in the clouds." Among those in a shaman's service, this spirit is said to have been one of the most powerful and feared.

65.
SHAMAN'S CHARM, HAIDA
bone, haliotis, cedar bark, 17.2 cm. l.

Collected by A. A. Aronson in 1882 on Queen Charlotte Island. Purchased from James Terry in 1891. This is a soul-catcher charm, used by a shaman to capture the soul from an ailing patient. The cedar bark stoppers with which it was originally equipped are still in place. The considerable wear of this example suggests that it was a heirloom and that it was used by several generations of shamans.

Shaman's Charms

Shamans' charms were made of a variety of materials including wood, bone, bear teeth, antler and shell. Walrus and whale ivory, both obtained by trade with the Eskimos, was also commonly used. Some charms were worn as pendants. Others formed parts of necklaces, and yet another type was sewn on to dance capes. They were carved to represent animal spirits that aided a shaman and were used to effect cures or bring success in such activities as hunting, fishing, or warfare. A shaman would sometimes touch a charm to the ailing part of the body of a sick patient to bring about a cure. Many charms represent easily identifiable animals, but others take the form of supernatural spirits such as might have appeared to the shaman in a vision.

A particular type of charm, known as a soul catcher, is a tube carved of bone or occasionally of wood that was originally fitted with a bark stopper at each end. It was worn as a pendant by the shaman in curing ceremonies when it was believed that the soul of an ailing person had departed from his body. Only the shaman was able to locate the soul. He followed it, often chanting and repeating incantations until he was able to catch it in the charm. The soul was then returned to the patient who was expected to recover from his illness.

During some curing ceremonies the shaman wore a crown. These were usually made of bear claws but other materials including mountain goat horn, wood and bone were also used. The shaman would rub the body of an ailing patient with the crown to aid recovery.

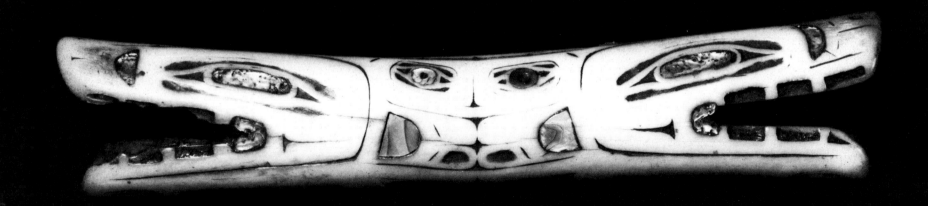

66.
SHAMAN'S CHARM, TLINGIT
bone, 7.1 cm. h.

Collected by G. T. Emmons between 1884-93 from a shaman's grave house near Gan-dar-kan village. The large head is that of a wolf, and devilfish tentacles appear at the ears. The seated figure at the back of the charm is a bear.

67.
SHAMAN'S CHARM, TLINGIT
ivory, 12.5 cm. h.

Collected by G. T. Emmons between 1884-93 from the grave house of a shaman of the Gunnah-ho clan on the "Towtuck" river between Yakutat and Dry Bay. Emmons interprets the figures as follows: the central animal is a bear devouring a Tlingit and grasping another with its left paw. Below is a devilfish spirit, and above is a whale spirit. The bird figures on the left and right represent sand hill cranes. This charm is said to have passed through several generations of practicing shamans.

66

67

68.
COMB, TLINGIT
wood, haliotis, 13.2 cm. h.

Purchased from G. T. Emmons in 1926. The large figure is a beaver.

69.
SHAMAN'S CROWN, TLINGIT
mountain sheep horn, animal hide, dentalium, puffin beak, twine, 17.5 cm. h.

Collected by G. T. Emmons between 1882-87 at Chilkat.

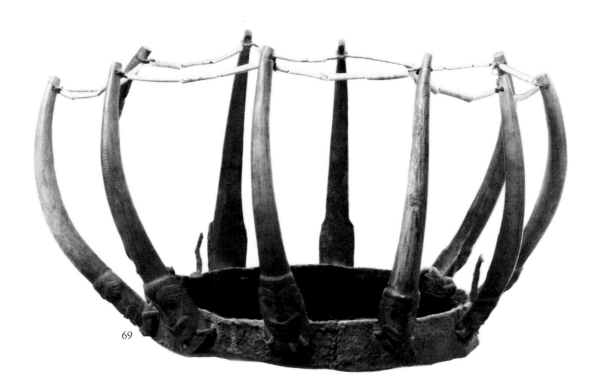

69

68

Bowls, Boxes and Chests

On the Northwest Coast, boxes were used for many different purposes and were made in a variety of sizes. They served as coffins, cremation chests, drums, quivers, tackle boxes, storage chests, shamans' medicine boxes, food bowls and cooking vessels. Only the large coffins and cremation chests were made out of a single piece of wood that was hollowed out.

The smaller boxes were all constructed in the same way. They were invariably made of cedar, and the sides were carved from one plank of wood which was kerfed, steamed and bent at the corners. The first and fourth sides were then sewn or pegged together, and the bottoms were attached separately with pegs.

Food boxes were used as vessels for serving fish and other food to guests at feasts. Usually these have slightly bulging sides which were carved in relief with designs representing family crests. Closely related is a watertight box often called a grease bowl. It held candlefish oil which was served at feasts as a condiment for dried fish, berries or seaweed. The top sides of these boxes were carved to bend inward to prevent spilling.

Storage chests are large, horizontal, rectangular boxes. Most often, they were carved in relief on the front and back, and painted on the sides. The front is usually more elaborately carved and decorated than the back. The designs are sometimes inlaid and represent family crests. They were always made with a top and were used to store such significant family possessions as blankets, ceremonial costumes, crest helmets, rattles, masks, furs and ceremonial coppers. The chests themselves were often regarded as important family heirlooms, and they were sometimes carved and painted by professional artists. The Indians believed that such chests were inhabited and protected by the spirits of the animals that were represented in the decorations.

Another type of rectangular storage box was made to stand vertically. It held various household possessions such as blankets and clothing, but was not used for objects of such great importance as were placed in the chests. The most common examples were painted with red and black pigments by their owners, with stylized crest designs. Bold and abstract animal crests were painted on the front and back, and smaller and simpler motifs were often painted on the sides. Some examples were carved on all four sides. Although many of these boxes have survived and certain designs appear similar, none have been found to be exactly the same. These boxes often have tops ornamented with shell, inlaid in simple geometric patterns, but painted or carved designs were never applied to the tops.

70.
COFFIN, HAIDA
wood, red, green and black
pigment, 67.0 cm. h.,
160.0 cm. l.

*Collected by C.F. Newcombe in
1901 at Skedans. Newcombe
identifies the design on the
front as representing the moon
with the head of a bird in the
center, and the large carving on
the back as the head of a mountain goat. The two figures at the
ends are grizzly bears. In a letter
to Boas, dated May 9, 1901,
Newcombe writes, "I have also
agreed to buy a large carved
yellow cedar coffin made more
than twenty years ago by the
late Skedans (a Haida Chief) . . .
for himself, but considered by
his survivors as more suitable as
a receptacle for blankets."*

70

71

71.
BOX, BELLA BELLA
wood, operculum, rawhide,
twine, red, black and blue
pigment, 21.7 cm. h.

Collected by I. W. Powell in
1881, H. R. Bishop Collection.

72.
CHEST, TSIMSHIAN
wood, rawhide, traces of red and
black pigment, 49.3 cm. h.

Collected by G. T. Emmons in
1909 from the second chief of
the village of Kitwanga, Upper
Skeena River. Emmons inter-
prets the design on the front as
representing a bear, that on the
back as a sea bear and those
painted on the sides as a beaver
and a bear.

72

73

73.
BOX, TLINGIT
wood, red and black pigment,
45.5 cm. h.

Collected by G. T. Emmons
between 1882-87 at Chilkat.
Emmons interprets the design
as representing a seal. William
Reid has suggested that the
motif is a bird form. The paint-
ing is unusual in its complexity
and the inclusion of the areas of
red over black designs.

74.
BOX, TLINGIT
wood, spruce root, traces of red
and blue pigment, 37.5 cm. h.

Collected by G. T. Emmons be-
tween 1884-93 from the grave
house of a shaman named
Chyeeke. Emmons identifies
the design as representing a
water spirit and states that the
box held the shaman's
implements.

74

75.
CHEST, TLINGIT
wood, operculum, copper,
spruce root, traces of red and
black pigment, 49.3 cm. h.

Collected by G. T. Emmons between 1884-93 at Klukwan. Emmons's notes describe this box as having been the property of Shartrich, a Tlingit chief who accompanied the first Russian visitors to the area up the Chilkat River in 1834. In 1852, according to information from Edmund Carpenter, (1975, p. 16), he led a party of Tlingit to Fort Selkirk to burn the Hudson's Bay Company post. The chest was part of the furnishings of the Whale House of the Chilkat and appears in an early photograph of the interior. The figures of three bears, two in profile, appear on the front of the box. Early boxes of this type are known as "telescope boxes." A smaller, undecorated box is in the inside, and when it is opened, the sides and top are lifted off together.

75

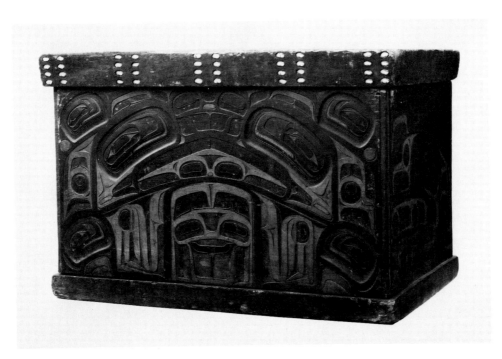

76.
CHEST, TLINGIT
wood, operculum, haliotis, red,
blue and black pigment,
54.0 cm. h.

Collected by G. T. Emmons
between 1884-93 at Klukwan.
Emmons interprets the design
as representing a mythical
water spirit.

76

77

78

77.
BENT BOWL, TLINGIT
wood, operculum, haliotis,
twine, red, black and blue
pigment, 16.5 cm. h.

Collected by G. T. Emmons be-
tween 1882-87 at Chilkat. The
carving represents a brown bear.

78.
DISH, HAIDA
mountain sheep horn, 26.2 cm. l.

Collected by G. T. Emmons in
1885 at Yakutat. Although he
collected this piece in country
inhabited by the Tlingit,
Emmons states that the dish is
Haida and at one time belonged
to chiefs of the Stikine clan. He
identifies the figures at each end
as owls, but it is more likely
they are hawks.

79.
OIL DISH, HAIDA
wood, 28.0 cm. l.

Collected by G. T. Emmons
between 1884-93. The dish is in
the form of a hair seal.

80.
FEAST BOWL, TLINGIT
wood, operculum, black, blue
and red pigment, 66.0 cm. l.

Collected by G. T. Emmons be-
tween 1882-87 at Chilkat. Two
bear figures are carved at each end.

79

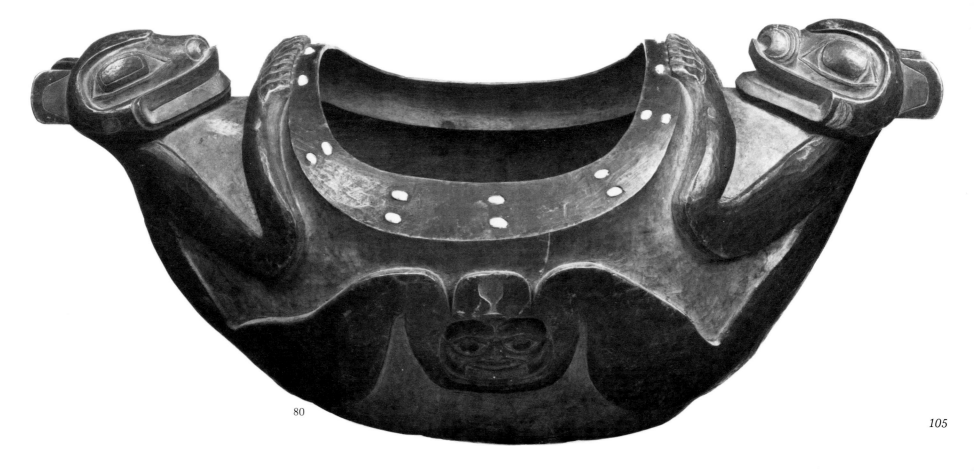

80

FEAST DISH, KWAKIUTL
wood, red pigment, 76.0 cm. l.

Collected by G. Hunt in 1901.
A killer whale is represented.
This bowl is one of a pair.

81

82.
CHEST FRONT, KWAKIUTL
wood, red and black pigment,
54.0 cm. h.
Collected by G. Hunt in 1899 at
Fort Rupert.

82

83.
RELIEF PANEL, TLINGIT
wood, operculum, black, traces
of red pigment, 48.0 cm. h.

Collected by G. T. Emmons between 1884-93 at Sitka. This piece with a relief in the form of a bear head originally was in the front of a platform in a chief's house. Emmons identifies the house as having been owned by the Kar-guan-ton clan of the Tlingit.

83

Spoons and Ladles

Spoons were the common eating implement on the Northwest Coast. Numerous undecorated examples were owned and used for everyday purposes. Only the decorated feast spoons are included in this exhibition.

One type is made from wood, usually alder, and is decorated with crest designs painted in red and black pigments on the inside of the bowl. On some examples, the handle is also carved in the round with animal forms.

Horn spoons are more common. Each important family had a supply of these and the number a family owned would indicate something of the size of the feast the family could give. The mountain goat horn handles represent family crests, and have much of the same form and symbolism as totem poles. The bowl was made by boiling the horn in water or exposing it to steam until it became soft. It was then placed in a two part wooden mold which was tied together, allowing the horn to harden into the desired shape as it cooled. The handle was also softened in a similar way and bent into the proper curve. After shaping, the handle and sometimes the outer portion of the bowl were carved and incised. Shell inlays were also often added, and parts of the handle were occasionally made of bone or ivory. Because of the small size of each piece of goat horn, the bowl of the spoon was usually molded separately and attached to the handle with horn or metal rivets. Some examples have sheep horn bowls affixed to goat horn handles. Both types of horn were obtained locally or through trade with other Indian groups who lived in the interior.

A rarer form of spoon is the flat, wood, soapberry spoon. These are carved with relief designs and are in the form of a long spatula with a handle. They were used to eat a mash made of soapberries which was served only on important occasions as soapberries were difficult to obtain and prepare.

Ladles were used at feasts to serve oil and food from feast dishes. Some very large examples were made of wood and carved with animal forms on the handle. A smaller and more common variety was made of mountain sheep horn by the same techniques as were used to make the horn spoons. Because sheep horns are large, the entire ladle is one piece of horn. Some examples are completely unadorned while others have elaborate crest designs on the handle and the outside of the bowl.

84.
SPOON, TLINGIT
mountain goat horn, copper, 25.5 cm. l.
Collected by G. T. Emmons between 1882-87 at Chilkat. A crane head is at the top, and a human figure crouches over a frog on the lower part of the handle.

85.
SPOON, TLINGIT
mountain goat horn, metal, 23.5 cm. l.
Given in memory of Major and Mrs. Junius MacMurray by Mrs. J. Marvin Wright in 1946.

86.
SPOON, TLINGIT
mountain goat horn, metal, 20.8 cm. l.
Gift of Thomas Ransom, 1935. The handle is in the form of a raven with a crouching human figure below.

84

85

86

87

87.
LADLE, TLINGIT
mountain sheep horn,
54.5 cm. l.

*Collected by G. T. Emmons
between 1882-87 at Chilkat. A
raven head decorates the end.*

88.
LADLE, TLINGIT
mountain sheep horn, haliotis,
43.3 cm. l.

*Gift of J. G. Phelps Stokes in
1906. Below the raven head at
the top are figures of a human
and frog.*

89.
SOAPBERRY SPOON, TLINGIT
wood, 36.3 cm. l.

*Collected by G. T. Emmons be-
tween 1882-87 from Annette
Island. The spoon is carved in
the form of a dogfish.*

88

89

90.
FEAST LADLE, HAIDA
wood, metal staples, red and
black pigment, 102.0 cm. l.

Gift of Mrs. Albert Bierstadt in
1905. The bird has been iden-
tified as a loon or cormorant.

90

**91.
CEREMONIAL FOOD TRAY,
TLINGIT**
wood, operculum, 93.2 cm. l.

Collected by G. T. Emmons between 1882-87 at Wrangell. Emmons's notes identify the carving at each end as representing an "old and young brown bear." He also states that the tray was the property of a chief who died in 1879.

Daggers

Before contact some double-ended copper knives were made and owned by chiefs. With the appearance of the white man and the availability of iron, the Indians developed a wide variety of knives and metal implements for carving, skinning and butchering. In the early nineteenth century, the dagger was an important weapon. With the introduction of firearms, the dagger gradually came to be used as a status symbol. It was worn in a sheath that hung from the neck and carried in front of the wearer. The blades were forged and usually made of iron from files or bars. Crest designs carved in wood, bone, horn, or ivory and often inlaid with haliotis shell decorated the hilts.

92.
DAGGER, HAIDA
iron, hair, rawhide, bone,
40.2 cm. l.

Collected by G. T. Emmons between 1884-93. On the handle, a bear holds a human figure, and a raven head appears at the top. Emmons identifies the small figure between the bear paws as a blackfish.

92

93.
PIPE, TLINGIT
wood, iron, 19.7 cm. h.

Collected by G. T. Emmons between 1882-87 "at Kon Island." An eagle is represented.

93

Pipes

Before the coming of European, Russian and American traders, the Northwest Coast Indians cultivated a tobacco-like plant that was chewed. When tobacco was introduced in the early nineteenth century, it was often mixed with pieces of shredded cedar bark and smoked in pipes, used only by men. Carved pipes were made of imported hardwood with copper or brass bowls. Some pipes were also made of stone. The carvings were usually in the form of crest designs.

94.
PIPE, TLINGIT
wood, copper and brass,
17.4 cm. l.

Collected by G. T. Emmons between 1884-93 at Sitka. The hardwood that forms the bowl is not indigenous to the Northwest Coast and was probably brought in by traders. Emmons describes the many figures on this pipe as follows: "On either side of the bowl is carved a raven and a sea otter, underneath the bowl is represented a dogfish and a sculpin, on the stem is a sand hill crane with [its] bill in the mouth of a frog. The brass cap is engraved as an eagle, and the ornamental brass cap on the bowl is engraved as a sea otter."

94

Halibut Hooks

These fishhooks were kept in place by a float and sinker and were designed to hang horizontally in the water. The barbed leg of the hook was wrapped with bait of octopus or squid tentacle and, after the halibut took it, the spike pierced its lip as it backed away. The part of the hook that faced the bottom was carved so that it would be seen by the fish. Usually the sculpture represents a creature known for its ability to catch fish. Each hook had its own name and before it was used it was addressed by the fisherman to bring success. Many examples are of crude workmanship because they were probably carved by their owners and their efficiency in catching fish was regarded as more important than any aesthetic considerations.

95.
HALIBUT HOOK, TLINGIT
wood, spruce root strips, iron
and black pigment, 26.5 cm. l.

Gift of Mary Sayre in memory
of Reginald Sayre in 1932.

95

96.
TOTEM POLE CARVING, HAIDA
slate, 53.7 cm. h.
Collected by I. W. Powell in 1881, H. R. Bishop Collection.

97.
BLANKET PIN, HAIDA
silver, 9.1 cm. h.
Collected by G. Kung before 1907. Gift of Mrs. H. Zinsser in 1951. The design is in the form of a beaver.

98.
BOX FRONT, HAIDA
slate, 13.7 cm. h.
Purchased from S. Kirschberg, Victoria, B. C. in 1896. The design represents a bear.

99.
BOWL, HAIDA
slate, 37.0 cm. d.
Collected by I. W. Powell in 1881, H. R. Bishop Collection. Boas identifies the figure as a sea monster.

Slate and Silver

Around 1820 the Haida Indians began to carve a dense carbonaceous shale into objects that were sold to visiting traders. The stone, often called argillite, comes from one quarry on Queen Charlotte Island near Skidegate and no other sources are known on the coast. This type of shale is soft and can be worked with the same tools that were used to carve wood. Many of the pieces were made in traditional shapes and with characteristic Northwest Coast designs. There is also a large body of work that was made specifically for the white man's taste and includes representations of sea captains, their ships and numerous motifs borrowed from Russian, American or European decorative art. Such objects as pipes, boxes, plates, free standing figures and models of totem poles were made from slate.

Another material that came to be used by Northwest Coast artists in the nineteenth century was silver which was worked from silver dollars. The art of engraving silver is thought to have been introduced by Russians around 1800 at Sitka. The Indians made bracelets, pins and ornaments for their own use and also produced silver cane handles, napkin rings and jewelry for commercial purposes.

98

97

99

100.
MEMORIAL POST, HAIDA
wood, red, black, white and
green pigment, 248.0 cm. h.
Collected by I. W. Powell in
1881, H. R. Bishop Collection.
The figure represents a beaver.

Memorial Poles

Large scale animal form carvings were erected by the heir in
the family of a deceased chief to show he had assumed the
family crests and titles. The successor had the memorial pole
carved and set up in front of his village for all to see. Usually
such poles are in the form of a single animal representing the
most important family crest.

100

This bibliography relates only to specific references that are made in the catalogue. For a more complete bibliography on the subject of Northwest Coast Art, see Wardwell, A. and Lebov, L., 1970.

Berkeley, Robert H. Lowie Museum
  1965 *Art of the Northwest Coast*, Robert H. Lowie Museum of Anthropology, University of California, Berkely.

Boas, Franz
  1898 "The Mythology of the Bella Coola Indians," *American Museum of Natural History Memoirs*, No. 2, part 2, Jesup Expedition, New York.

Boas, Franz
  1909 "The Kwakiutl of Vancouver Island," *American Museum of Natural History Memoirs*, No. 8, part 2, Jesup Expedition, 5, New York, pp. 307-516.

Boas, Franz
  1927 "Primitive Art," *Instituttet for Sammenlignende Kulturforskning*, VII, series B, Oslo. Many later editions.

Carpenter, Edmund
  1975 "Collecting Northwest Coast Art," *Form and Freedom: A Dialogue on Northwest Coast Indian Art*, Rice University, Houston.

Chicago, The Art Institute of Chicago
  1964 *Yakutat South, Indian Art of the Northwest Coast*, Chicago.

Covarrubias, Miguel
  1954 *The Eagle, the Jaguar and the Serpent*, Alfred A. Knopf, New York.

Dawson, George M.
  1878 "Report on the Queen Charlotte Islands," *Geological Survey of Canada*, Report on Progress, Appendix A, Montreal.

Douglas, Frederick and d'Harnoncourt, Rene
  1941 *Indian Art of the United States*, The Museum of Modern Art, New York.

Drucker, Philip
  1955 *Indians of the Northwest Coast*, Anthropological Handbook, American Museum of Natural History, New York.

de Laguna, Frederica
  1972 "Under Mount Saint Elias: the History and Culture of the Yakutat Tlingit," *Smithsonian Contributions to Anthropology*, Volume 7 (in three parts), Washington, D.C.

Duff, Wilson
  1967 "Contexts of Northwest Coast Art," *Arts of the Raven*, Vancouver Art Gallery, Vancouver.

Emmons, George T.
  1916 "The Whale House of the Chilkat," *American Museum of Natural History Journal*, XVI, no. 7, pp. 451-460.

Emmons, George T.
  1930 "The Art of the Northwest Coast Indians," *Natural History*, Vol. XXX, American Museum of Natural History, New York, pp. 282-292.

Emmons, George T. and Boas, Franz
  1907 "The Chilkat Blanket, with notes on Blanket Designs," *American Museum of Natural History Memoirs*, No. 3, part 4, New York, pp. 329-400.

Feder, Norman
  1971a *American Indian Art*, Harry N. Abrams, Inc., New York.

Feder, Norman
  1971b *Two Hundred Years of North American Indian Art*, Praeger Publishers, New York.

Feder, Norman and Malin, E.
  1962 "Indian Art of the Northwest Coast," *Indian Leaflet Series*, Nos. 148-171, Denver Art Museum, Denver.

Fraser, Douglas
  1962 *Primitive Art*, Doubleday, Garden City.

Goddard, Pliny Earle
   1934   "Indians of the Northwest Coast" *Handbook No.10*, American Museum of Natural History, New York.

Gunther, Erna
   1966   *Art in the Life of the Northwest Coast Indian*, The Portland Art Museum, Portland.

Gunther, Erna
   1972   *Indian Life on the Northwest Coast of North America*, University of Chicago Press, Chicago.

Hawthorne, Audrey
   1967   *Art of the Kwakiutl Indians*, University of British Columbia, Museum, Vancouver.

Holm, Bill
   1965   *Northwest Coast Indian Art*, University of Washington Press, Seattle.

Holm, Bill
   1972   *Crooked Beak of Heaven*, University of Washington Press, Seattle.

Holm, Bill and Reid, William
   1975   *Form and Freedom: A Dialogue on Northwest Coast Indian Art*, Rice University, Houston.

Inverarity, Robert Bruce
   1950   *Art of the Northwest Coast Indians*, University of California Press, Los Angeles.

Levi-Strauss, Claude
   1943   "Art of the Northwest Coast at the American Museum of Natural History," *Gazette des Beaux Arts*, XXIV, September, pp. 175-182.

Maurer, Evan
   The Native American Heritage, A Survey of North American Indian Art, The Art Institute of Chicago, Chicago.

Minneapolis, Walker Art Center
   1972   *American Indian Art: Form and Tradition*, Minneapolis.

National Gallery of Art
   1973   *The Far North: 2,000 Years of American Eskimo and Indian Art*, Washington, D.C.

Paris, Musee de L'Homme
   1969   *Chefs d'oeuvre des Arts Indiens et Esquimaux du Canada*.

Reid, William
   1967   "The Art—An Appreciation," *Arts of the Raven*, Vancouver Art Gallery, Vancouver.

Seattle, Seattle Worlds Fair
   1962   *Northwest Coast Indian Art*.

Siebert, Erna and Forman, W.
   1967   *Indianerkunst Der Amerikanischen Nordwestkuste*, Artice, Prague.

Sturtevant, William
   1974   *Boxes and Bowls*, Renwick Gallery, Washington, D.C.

Swanton, John R.
   1905   "The Haida of Queen Charlotte Island," *American Museum of Natural History, Memoirs*, 5, part 1, Jesup Expedition, New York.

Vaillant, George C.
   1939   *Indian Arts in North America*, Harpers, New York.

Vancouver, Vancouver Art Gallery
   1967   *Arts of the Raven*, Catalogue 426, Vancouver.

Wardwell, Allen and Lebov, Lois
   1970   *Annotated Bibliography of Northwest Coast Indian Art*, The Museum of Primitive Art, New York.

Appendix

The American Museum of Natural History's accession numbers and references to the object in other publications are noted below. Tribal attributions follow AMNH records.

1. 16/8912
Ref: Boas, F., 1909, pl. XLI, no. 6.

2. E 414
Ref: de Laguna, F., p. 1108, pl. 188, lower left.

3. E 410
Ref: de Laguna, F., p. 1109, pl. 189, right.

4. E 409
Ref: de Laguna, F., p. 1108, pl. 188, top right.

5. 19/850
Ref: Minneapolis, no. 605; Vancouver, no. 39.

6. E 342
Ref: de Laguna, F., p. 1098, pl. 180, top left.

7. E 343
Ref: de Laguna, F., p. 1098, pl. 180, bottom left; Minneapolis, no. 608.

8. E 2683

9. 16.1/996
Ref: Minneapolis, no. 610.

10. E 2486
Ref: de Laguna, F., p. 1105, pl. 186, lower left.

11. 19/892
Ref: Minneapolis, no. 602.

12. 19/854
Ref: Feder, N., 1971a, pl. 152; Minneapolis, no. 609.

13. 16.1/621
Ref: Chicago, no. 71.

14. 19/864
Ref: Minneapolis, no. 601.

15. E 725
Ref: Minneapolis, no. 455.

16. 19/997

17. E 1598

18. E 2364
Ref: Minneapolis, no. 446.

19. 19/917
Ref: Chicago, no. 48.

20. 19/916
Ref: Minneapolis, no. 439.

21. E 2372
Ref: Minneapolis, no. 450.

22. 19/920
Ref: Boas, F., 1927, p. 218, fig. 209; Chicago, no. 37; Minneapolis, no. 436.

23. 16/264

24. 19/890
Ref: Minneapolis, no. 579.

25. 16/594
Ref: Feder, N., 1971a, colorplate 39; 1971b, no. 40; Swanton, J. R., pl. XXV, no. 5; Goddard, P., p. 150, ill.

26. 19/898

27. 16/6757

28. 16/976
Ref: Boas, F., 1895, p. 3; 1909, pl. XLV, no. 1; Drucker, P., pl. 90 d. (These illustrations show the entire monument).

29. 16/963
Ref: Berkeley, p. 67, ill.

30. 16/2346

31. 19/897

32. E 1062

33. E 1560

34. 19/995
Ref: Feder, N., 1971b, no. 92.

35. 16/2359
Ref: Boas, F., 1909, pl. LI, 1, 2, and p. 521; Drucker, P., pl. 80; Chicago, no. 52.

36. 16/1101
Ref: Boas, F., 1895, pl. 30, figs. 1, 2.

37. 16/1508

38. 16/8273
Ref: Boas, F., 1909, pl. XLII; 1927, fig. 198d; Chicago, no. 57.

39. 16/8384
Ref: Boas, F., 1909, pl. 39; 1927, p. 208, fig. 198.

40. 16/2362
Ref: Boas, F., 1909, pl. L11.

41. 16/280
Ref: Berkeley, p. 69, ill.

42. AMNH 78

43. 16/1443
ref: Boas, F., 1898, pl. XI, 1.

44. 16/9014

45. 16/1506
Ref: Berkeley, p. 73, ill.; Minneapolis, no. 571, ill.; Drucker, P., pl. 98, left.

46. 16/596
Ref: Feder, N., 1969, colorplate no. 40; 1971, no. 53; Vancouver, no. 14.

47. E 1580

48. 16/952

Ref: Emmons, G. T., 1907, pl. XXVI.

49. 16/351
Ref: Emmons, G. T. and Boas, F., fig. 546 b; Boas, F., 1927, p. 214, fig. 204; Vancouver, no. 317.

50. 19/803
Ref: Minneapolis, no. 731; Vancouver, no. 70.

51. 16/942
Ref: Minneapolis, no. 862.

52. E 421
Ref: de Laguna, F., p. 1107, pl. 187, bottom right.

53. E 1373

54. 16/9378

55. 19/806
Ref: Vancouver, no. 65.

56. 16.1/1909

57. 16/9379
Ref: Drucker, P., pl. 70b; Minneapolis, no. 737.

58. 19/259
Ref: Berkeley, p. 24, ill.

59. 19/334

60. 19/337
Ref: Boas, F., 1927, p. 199, fig. 183.

61. 19/378
Ref: Chicago, no. 106; Fraser, D., pl. 179; National Gallery of Art, no. 285, ill., p. 229; Berkeley, ill., p. 61.

62. 19/308

63. 19/258

64. 19/450

65. T 22644
Ref: Drucker, P., pl. 75c (here attributed to Tlingit).

66. E 2711

67. E 2708
Ref: Vaillant, G., pl. 92.

68. 16.1/1795

69. 19/1010

70. 16/8802
Ref: Swanton, J. R., p. 132, fig. 12; Goddard, P., ill., p. 150.

71. 16/945

72. 16.1/627

73. 19/1233
Ref: Boas, F., 1927, p. 276, fig. 287b; Emmons, G. T. and Boas, F., p. 364, fig. 558; Vancouver, no. 293, ill.

74. E 1579

75. E 2295

Ref: Emmons, G. T., 1916, fig. 6.

76. E 1237
Ref: Douglas F. and d'Harnoncourt, R., p. 178, ill.

77. 19/1086
Ref: Berkeley, p. 26, ill.

78. 19/696
Ref: Douglas, F. and d'Harnoncourt, R., p. 180, ill.; Goddard, P., ill., p. 155.

79. E 389

80. 19/1239
Ref: Vancouver, no. 298.

81. 16/8527
Ref: Boas, F., 1909, pl. XLIII; 1927, fig. 179 f.

82. 16/6923

83. E 1385
Ref: Feder, N. 1969, colorplate no. 38; 1971, no. 73; National Gallery of Art, no. 132, ill., p. 184.

84. 19/1123

85. 16.1/2375

86. 16.1/1990

87. 19/1109

88. 16.1/368

89. E 2502

90. 16.1/339

91. E 1383

92. E 2067
Ref: Berkeley, p. 62, ill.; Vancouver, no. 241; Minneapolis, no. 852.

93. 19/685
Ref: Berkeley, p. 23, ill.

94. E 2406

95. 16.1/1936
Ref: Drucker, P., fig. 6, top.

96. 16/555

97. 16.1/2538
Ref: Feder, N., 1969, no. 163, ill.

98. 16/1150

99. 16/611
Ref: Boas, F., 1927, p. 246, fig. 258.

100. 16/569